Copyright Essentials

FOR

Librarians

AND

Educators

KENNETH D. CREWS

A PROJECT OF THE COPYRIGHT MANAGEMENT CENTER

Indiana University–Purdue University Indianapolis

WITH CONTRIBUTIONS FROM

Dwayne K. Buttler

Rebecca Parman

Barbara Gushrowski

Noemí Rivera-Morales

Mary Jane Frisby

John O'Donnell

AMERICAN LIBRARY ASSOCIATION

Chicago and London   2000

Dedication . . .

In honor of

Judy L. Homer

who now pursues even greater ambitions,
but whose creative services to the
Copyright Management Center
made the original tutorial possible

Printed on 50-pound white offset, a pH-neutral stock, and bound in 10-point cover stock by Data Reproduction

The paper used in this publication meets the minimum requirements of American National Standard for Information Sciences—Permanence of Paper for Printed Library Materials, ANSI Z39.48-1992. ∞

Library of Congress Cataloging-in-Publication Data

Crews, Kenneth D.
    Copyright essentials for librarians and educators / Kenneth D. Crews with contributions from Dwayne K. Buttler ... [et al.].
      p. cm.
  ISBN 0-8389-0797-0
    1. Copyright—United States. 2. Librarians—United States—Handbooks, manuals, etc. 3. Teachers—United States—Handbooks, manuals, etc. I. Title

  KF2995 .C74 2001
  346.7304′82′024092—dc21   00-059421

Printed in the United States of America.

04 03 02 01 00   5 4 3 2 1

Contents

Fair Use

Special Exceptions

Looking Ahead

Appendices

1

Introduction:
Background and Acknowledgments

Rapid changes in the nature of scholarship and communications have drawn greater attention to the vital relationship between copyright law and the success of teaching, research, and library services. Copyright law helps entrepreneurs to become multi-millionaires and thousands of teachers, scholars, readers, and librarians to meet their goals each day. As more of us create new works and share them widely on the Internet, we are concerned about protecting our own rights. As we use works created by others in innovative and often high-profile ways, we are sometimes left to struggle with complex issues of fair use. Moreover, new statutes, such as the Digital Millennium Copyright Act, raise unexpected complications and promise to restructure owners' rights and impede the application of fair use.

This book is designed to introduce copyright fundamentals to busy and sophisticated educators and information professionals by means of a series of succinct, explanatory units focused on common needs and situations—and on discrete aspects of the law. A central purpose of this work is to help readers grasp the meaning of copyright law in the context of a professional commitment to advancing and disseminating knowledge. In that spirit, a little knowledge can help manage the external influences of copyright and often turn them to one's advantage. You do not need to become an expert, but a little knowledge can be a valuable asset. Knowledge can help you scale obstacles, resolve challenges, and more successfully meet goals.

Relative to the growing body of copyright law, this book is ultimately only a "little knowledge." Moreover, this project focuses on American copyright law and is relevant principally to the creation and use of copyrighted works inside the jurisdiction of the United States. With the "harmonization" of copyright laws around the world, however, many broad tenets of American law have comparable counterparts in other countries. Yet the expansion of international trade and the growth of worldwide computer networks may trigger your need to reach beyond domestic principles and to learn the laws of other nations.

1

Origins of the Online Copyright Tutorial

This book is a direct outgrowth of the Online Copyright Tutorial that I developed in association with the Copyright Management Center (CMC) at Indiana University Purdue-University Indianapolis (IUPUI). The first tutorial was offered in spring 1998, with an updated and refined version in fall 1998. Those tutorials were a series of brief and readable email messages delivered to subscribers around the world. With relatively little publicity, the first offering had more than 2,200 subscribers; the second had more than 2,500.

The Online Copyright Tutorial was a manifestation of one of the most important objectives of the CMC: to educate the library and academic communities about copyright. The CMC has solved problems, answered questions, drafted documents, and developed policy. Yet education has been its most critical and effective pursuit. Education can reach a wide array of individuals simultaneously and prepare them for the unpredictable innovations of the future. In that spirit, this book is an educational tool for the widest possible audience of librarians and educators.

In spring 2000 the CMC once again offered the Online Copyright Tutorial, this time in association with the American Library Association (ALA). Carrie Russell, copyright specialist in ALA's Office for Information Technology Policy in Washington, D.C., invited the CMC to develop an abbreviated version of the tutorial for ALA members, emphasizing fair use and other issues of greatest importance to librarians. The American Association of Law Libraries (AALL) joined in supporting the effort.

The new version addressed extraordinary developments from the preceding eighteen months. In late 1998 Congress enacted the Digital Millennium Copyright Act and the Sonny Bono Copyright Term Extension Act. Courts around the country were also handing down an increasing number of decisions affecting new media and Internet applications. The new version of the tutorial reached more than 6,500 subscribers. Many subscribers asked for a published compilation of the tutorial messages; I hope that this book fulfills that need and more.

Updates, Supplements, and Resources

This book reflects the best of the Online Copyright Tutorials, with additional and even more recent information. The book's structure and content begin with the most complete tutorial from 1998, with updates of developments through the first half of 2000. Each chapter is fundamentally a revised and current version of one of the original tutorial messages, preserving its succinct, readable, and informal delivery. In addition, margin sidebars on each page offer numerous supplemental boxes that expand on the basic text with recent developments—new legislation, important cases, and events in the news. Readers can therefore draw from the basic text the essential information about each aspect of copyright law. Readers looking for more details and the latest developments can turn to the update boxes.

The use of supplemental boxes has an additional effect: each one emphasizes that copyright law has a depth of complexity and is constantly changing. Acts of Congress and judicial rulings constantly refine principles and sometimes overhaul them. Readers must stay attuned to news about copyright, and many new developments of importance to educators and librarians are summarized at the CMC website: <http://www.iupui.edu/~copyinfo>.

Readers will also find much more in this book than the Online Copyright Tutorial could offer. The appendices include a reading list for further information about all of the fundamental issues raised throughout the book. The appendices also include several of the more detailed summaries, papers, and resources developed by the CMC. Perhaps most significant among those materials is the "Checklist for Fair Use," a tool to help librarians, educators, and others work with fair use and make responsible decisions. The checklist is built upon a long series of court rulings that have analyzed and applied fair-use law and identified variables that can tip each of the four factors toward or away from a finding of fair use.

Naturally, any summary of fair use risks oversimplification, and a checklist built on a series of labels is hardly immune from criticism. Yet the checklist has been one of the most popular and useful projects of the CMC. It has been deployed by numerous individuals not only at our home institution, but also at colleges, universities, and libraries throughout the country. It has drawn favorable attention from authors, publishers, and many other parties sharing an interest in and concern about fair use. I hope it will continue to be useful to readers of this book; however, you still need to read and learn a little bit about fair use to make the checklist most effective. This book should offer that foundation.

Acknowledgments

The existence of this book has been possible only with the support of numerous individuals. Dwayne Buttler, an attorney and professional staff member at the CMC, served as "project manager" to take the work through multiple reviews, to coordinate contributions and corrections, and to bring the work to its final state. Rebecca Parman, administrative assistant at the CMC, has been instrumental in preparing multiple drafts and laboriously exploring software and layout options to develop clear, readable, and useful format for the text, update boxes, and appendices. Three current and former graduate students at Indiana

University—Noemí Rivera-Morales, Mary Jane Frisby, and Barbara Gushrowski—deployed their extraordinary talents to pursue research, prepare the updated reading list, critique and proofread the text, and unquestionably make the final book a vastly better resource. Ms. Rivera-Morales is a graduate student in the School of Library and Information Science; Ms. Frisby is a recent graduate of the School of Law-Indianapolis and will soon join the law firm of Barnes & Thornburg; Ms. Gushrowski is a graduate of our library school and is now a librarian with St. Vincent Hospital and Health Services and with Roche Diagnostics Corporation. I continue to be grateful for the contributions from John O'Donnell and Judy Homer who were part of the CMC at the inception of the Online Copyright Tutorial and who helped launched a project that led to the present book.

The CMC operates under the auspices of William Plater, Executive Vice Chancellor of IUPUI. His energy, creativity, initiative, and support brought the CMC into existence in 1994, and he has established an environment that encourages our best work. President Myles Brand of IU gave essential support to the CMC under his Strategic Directions Charter program, and his generous grant enabled us to expand our staffing during the last few years to pursue the tutorial, this book, and may other projects and services.

Special thanks go as well to Carrie Russell at ALA whose vision revived the tutorial in 2000, and to Patrick Hogan at ALA's publication offices who saw the opportunity to make this book possible. I extend my gratitude not only to these members of the CMC, IU, and ALA, but to their families, friends, and others who have given moral support when the deadlines pressed and when ambitions to innovate swelled. None of us works alone, and this book is clearly the product of a vast network of enthusiasts. The thanks go to them; the errors are all mine. I hope that the effort yields benefits for readers that match the devotion of the contributors.

Kenneth D. Crews
Indianapolis, Indiana
July 4, 2000

2

Why Is Copyright Important to You?

Copyright law is structured in a way that makes it directly relevant to many of the common and highly innovative teaching and research practices in libraries and educational institutions. Essentially, copyright law grants to the owners of the copyright a set of exclusive rights, including the right to make and distribute copies of the work. Each time you make and hand out copies of a protected article in class, for example, you are raising the possibility of having infringed the rights of the copyright owner.

Fortunately, the basic structure of the law then proceeds to carve out a number of exceptions to those rights. The best known of those exceptions is "fair use." The law also includes numerous other, more specific exceptions that are of immediate importance to education and librarianship. Among those exceptions are provisions for library copying,① performances and displays in classrooms or distance learning,② making backup copies of computer software,③ and making new formats of works for persons who are blind or who have other disabilities. Be careful about jumping to conclusions when using those exceptions; they are subject to rigorous conditions and limits. Later chapters in this book will examine most of these exceptions more closely.

The law also throws the net of copyright protection as broadly as possible. Copyright law now generously provides automatic protection for printed works, software, artworks, photographs and videos,

① The Digital Millennium Copyright Act (DMCA), enacted in October 1998, amended Section 108 of the 1976 Copyright Act to clarify that libraries could use digital technology for copies made for preservation or replacement purposes. Naturally, the "expansion" of opportunities comes with limits. Look for details in chapter 33.

② In the DMCA, Congress also directed the U.S. Copyright Office to conduct a study of the use of copyrighted works in digital distance education and to recommend changes in the statute that governs such uses. The Copyright Office delivered its report in May 1999. Chapter 31 examines the current law and the recommendations for change.

③ A recent case confirmed that under Section 117, one must be an "owner" and not a "licensee" of the computer software in order to exercise the benefits of Section 117. *DSC Comm. Corp. v. Pulse Comm. Inc.,* 170 F.3d 1354 (Fed. Cir. 1999).

and nearly everything you can find on the Internet. The term of protection is also extensive. In general, copyright lasts for a long time: the life of the author who creates the work, plus seventy years.④

Consequently, copyright applies to a wealth of materials. It applies to nearly everything that we might be using in our teaching and research, and it gives us protection for the new works that we create. Whether we realize it or not, we are in fact bumping up against copyright questions on a daily basis. If we do not manage them to our advantage, they will manage us and dictate how we conduct our scholarly work.

The two major multi-volume treatises on U.S. copyright law are:⑤

Goldstein, Paul. *Copyright*. 2d ed. 4 vols. New York: Aspen Law & Business, 2000.

Nimmer, Melville B. and David Nimmer. *Nimmer on Copyright*. 10 vols. New York: Matthew Bender & Co., 2000.

The full text of the U.S. Copyright Act is available from <http://lcweb.loc.gov/copyright/title17/>.⑥

④ The previous term of copyright was the life of the author, plus 50 years. In October 1998, Congress passed the Sonny Bono Term Extension Act, which extended the term of copyright by 20 years. Duration of copyright protection is the subject of chapters 10 and 11.

⑤ Constant updates bring these treatises current through at least the last several months.

⑥ Congress has enacted a number of new copyright bills during the last few years. The Copyright Act available on any website unfortunately may not always include the latest amendments. Consult with a law librarian to track any recent changes in the law.

3

What Works Are Protected by Copyright?

Copyright protects "original works of authorship" that are "fixed in any tangible medium of expression." This chapter will give a short overview of eligible works, and the next two chapters will provide more details about the concepts of "original works" and "fixed in a tangible medium of expression."

Copyrightable works include at least the following categories:

- Literary works
- Musical works, including any accompanying words
- Dramatic works, including any accompanying music
- Pantomimes and choreographic works
- Pictorial, graphic, and sculptural works
- Motion pictures and other audiovisual works
- Sound recordings
- Architectural works

These categories should be viewed quite broadly: for example, computer programs are "literary works"; maps are "pictorial, graphic, and sculptural works."

Once a work fits the "original" and "fixed" requirements for eligibility, how does one "get copyright protection" for that work? The answer may surprise you, and is addressed in chapters 8 and 9.

Sources

Section 102 of the U.S. Copyright Act. The full text is reprinted at appendix A2.

U.S. Copyright Office. *Copyright Basics, Circular 1.* Washington, D.C., 1998. Available from <http://lcweb.loc.gov/copyright/circs/circ01.pdf>.

For further information

Andorka, Frank H. *What Is a Copyright?* Chicago: American Bar Association, Section of Patent, Trademark and Copyright Law, 1992.

4

Eligibility for Copyright: What Is an "Original Work of Authorship"?

Copyright does not apply to everything; it applies only to "original works of authorship" that are "fixed in any tangible medium of expression." Courts give a broad reading to these concepts. This chapter examines the "original works" concept. The next chapter examines the "fixed" requirement.

Inspiration and Creativity

"Originality" is easily found in new writings, musical works, artwork, photography, and computer programming. You may also find originality in a new arrangement of existing facts or information. For example, scientific findings or facts may not be copyrightable,[1] but their arrangement on a table or their presentation in text may be protectable expression. Similarly, Homer's epic poems may never have had any legal protection in their first incarnation, but a new translation is an "original" work subject to new copyright protection. Fundamentally, originality in copyright means that the work came from your inspiration; you did not copy it from another source. Originality also implies some creativity.

[1] In an interesting case, a court recently held that information that appears to be "fact"—wholesale prices for collectible coins—may actually be copyrightable. Look for more information about this case in chapter 6.

Supreme Court Rulings

How original or creative must the work be? An original work must embody some "minimum amount of creativity." Courts have held that almost any spark of creativity beyond the "trivial" will constitute sufficient originality. In a famous 1903 case of a circus poster, Supreme Court Justice Holmes said that it was not for judges to decide the worth of pictorial illustrations. On the other hand, the U.S. Supreme Court ruled in 1991 that a "garden variety," alphabetical, white-pages telephone book[2] lacks the minimum creativity.[3]

Another example of necessary creativity is the case of a picture of Oscar Wilde. The court held that a photograph of Oscar Wilde did meet the requirement of creativity, because the photographer chose the camera, equipment, lighting, and where to stand to shoot the picture.[4]

Cases referenced in this message

Feist Publications, Inc. v. Rural Telephone Service Co., Inc., 499 U.S. 340 (1991) [phonebook case].

Bleistein v. Donaldson Lithographing Co., 188 U.S. 239 (1903) [circus poster case].

Burrow-Giles Lithographic Co. v. Sarony, 111 U.S. 53 (1884) [Oscar Wilde picture case].

For further information

Abrams, Howard B. "Originality and Creativity in Copyright Law." *Law & Contemporary Problems* 55 (Spring 1992): 3-44.

Leaffer, Marshall. *Understanding Copyright Law.* 3d ed. New York: Matthew Bender, 1999.

[2] Cases since 1991 have affirmed this ruling, but tested its limits. For example, a "yellow-pages" type listing may have sufficient originality in its categorization of information into subject headings. *Bellsouth Adver. & Publ. Corp. v. Donnelley Info Publ'g., Inc.*, 999 F.2d 1436 (11th Cir. 1993).

[3] This ruling has been of great concern to industries that invest significant funds to compile databases that may not be protected by U.S. copyright. Bills in Congress in recent years would establish a new form of legal protection for data compilations. Many educators and librarians have cautioned against these bills, arguing that they would add restraints on access to information. Arguments for and against proposals for database protection are available from the Database Data site <http://www.databasedata.org> and from the Digital Future Coalition site <http://www.dfc.org>.

[4] In *Bridgeman Art Library, Ltd. v. Corel Corp.*, 36 F. Supp.2d 191 (S.D.N.Y. 1999), the court ruled that a direct, accurate photographic reproduction of a two-dimensional artwork lacked sufficient creativity to be original. The work of art may still be protected by copyright, but the photograph may not. If the art is in the public domain, then no one may have a copyright interest in the image. Consistent with the Oscar Wilde case, however, if the photograph includes creative lighting, coloring, or angles, or captures more than just the work of art itself, then the photograph may easily qualify for copyright protection.

5

Eligibility for Copyright:
What Is "Fixed in a Tangible Medium of Expression"?

Is the sand castle that you and your nephew built at the beach last summer copyrightable? What about that beautiful ice sculpture you saw on New Year's Eve? The elegant Jell-O gelatin swan at the holiday party? More likely: how about that website you stored on a computer server?

Perceptible and Not Transitory

Each of these examples is more than likely an "original work of authorship," but to be eligible for copyright protection the work must also be "fixed" in some physical form capable of identification and having an existence of more than "transitory duration" that is not likely to disappear in a short time. Oozing gelatin might test the limits of copyrightability.

In addition, the fixed form does not have to be readable by the human eye, as long as the work can be perceived either directly or by a machine or device, such as a computer or projector. In other words, programming and substantive content stored on floppy disks or CDs are "fixed" as long as the works can be read with the use of a machine. A website is almost always "fixed."

Diverse Media

The "tangible medium" requirement expands copyright from traditional writings and pictures into the realm of video, sound recordings, computer disks, and Internet communications. If you can see it, read it, watch it, or hear it—with or without the use of a computer, projector, or other machine—the work is likely eligible for copyright protection. Hard questions surround the issue of whether materials stored only in the random-access memory (RAM) of a computer are sufficiently "fixed."[1] A fleeting appearance in RAM may not be enough, but once you hit the print or save key, that work is easily within copyright.

Given the wide range of media, and the broad scope of "originality" described in the previous message, the result is a vast array of works brought under the purview of copyright law.

For further information

Carter, Mary. *Electronic Highway Robbery: An Artist's Guide to Copyright in the Digital Era.* Berkeley: Peachpit Press, 1996.

Rose, Lance. *NetLaw: Your Rights in the Online World.* Berkeley: Osborne McGraw-Hill, 1995.

[1] An important case has held that software programming loaded into RAM was sufficiently stable to qualify as a "copy" for purposes of finding an infringement. The concept of a work in a stable medium for purposes of copying is similar to the standard used to determine if the work is "fixed" in the first place. See *MAI Sys. Corp. v. Peak Computer, Inc.*, 991 F.2d 511 (9th Cir. 1993).

6

What Works Are Not Protected by Copyright?

Copyright protects expression only—not ideas or facts. Therefore, if you tell someone your great idea for a book, and that person uses it for his or her own book, you are not likely to have a copyright claim. There is no copyright violation, although one might certainly find an ethical violation—or possibly breach of other legal rights.

Facts and discoveries are not protectable by copyright. You may have copyright protection for your original compilations of facts, but not for the facts themselves.[1] For example, many companies create and publish bibliographies and other factual compilations. The listings of authors' names, article titles, and the like are not protected, but the original arrangement of them into useful tools can be protected.

Several additional categories of material are generally not eligible for statutory copyright protection:

- Works that have not been fixed in a tangible form of expression. For example: choreographic works that have not been noted or recorded, or improvisational speeches or performances that have not been written or recorded.[2]

- Titles, names, short phrases, and slogans; familiar symbols or designs; mere variations

[1] The distinction between fact and a creative work is often unclear. A price on a product may appear to be "fact," but a court ruled recently that wholesale prices for collectible coins based on multivariable judgment calls and the appraiser's "best guess" are creative works protectable under copyright. *CDN, Inc. v. Kapes*, 197 F.3d 1256 (9th Cir. 1999).

[2] In a complicated twist, copyright law does not protect sound recordings, made without permission, of live performances of works. In 1994 Congress enacted legislation to protect against such "bootlegged" recordings. A recent court ruling holds that Congress can enact such legislation under its powers to regulate "interstate commerce," even though enacting the legislation may exceed congressional powers under the Copyright Clause of the United States Constitution. *U.S. v. Moghadam*, 175 F.3d 1269 (11th Cir. 1999), *cert. denied*, 120 S. Ct. 1529 (2000).

of typographic ornamentation, lettering, or coloring; mere listings of ingredients or contents.

- Ideas, procedures, methods, systems, processes, concepts, principles, discoveries, or devices, as distinguished from a description, explanation, or illustration.

- Works consisting entirely of information that is common property and containing no original authorship. For example: standard calendars, height and weight charts, tape measures and rulers, and lists or tables taken from public documents or other common sources.

Source

U.S. Copyright Office. *Copyright Basics, Circular 1*. Washington, D.C., 1998. Available from <http://lcweb.loc.gov/copyright/circs/circ01.pdf>.

For further information

Ginsburg, Jane C. "No 'Sweat?': Copyright and Other Protection of Works of Information after *Feist v. Rural Telephone*." *Columbia Law Review* 92 (March 1992): 338-88.

Kurtz, Leslie A. "Speaking to the Ghost: Idea and Expression in Copyright." *University of Miami Law Review* 47 (1993): 1221-61.

7

More Works That Cannot Be Copyrighted: U.S. Government Works

Scenario: You have just discovered a great source of information—the Consumer Information Catalog from Pueblo, Colorado. You have seen it advertised for years, but never knew there was anything useful in it. Can you use this material in your research project on consumer fraud without violating copyright?

Not So Simple

The United States government produces numerous works that are not copyrightable. A specific statute prohibits copyright protection for federal government works, but no rule is ever so simple. Reports written by members of Congress and employees of federal agencies, as part of their public function, are not copyrighted.[1] But projects written by non-government officials with federal funding may be copyright protected. For example, your research may be funded by government grants. The fact that you have a federal grant does not by itself put your work in the public domain; a government-funded project is not a "work of the United States Government."[2]

Similarly, just because a work is published by the federal government does not mean that it is therefore a government work and in the public domain. A publication from the Smithsonian Institution, for example, may well have been prepared by non-

[1] West Publishing long has published the full text of court opinions, and has sought innovative ways to assert legal control over the publications, even though the cases from federal courts are in the public domain. A recent ruling has confirmed that the text of the court decisions remains in the public domain, even if West has made corrections and other minor changes. *Matthew Bender & Co. v. West Publishing Co.*, 158 F.3d 674 (2d Cir. 1998).

[2] Section 105 of the Copyright Act sets forth the basic rule about government works, while Section 101 defines "work of the United States Government" as "a work prepared by an officer or employee of the United States Government as part of that person's official duties."

15

government authors and is therefore protectable by copyright. You need to examine each item closely, and inquire with the author or the issuing agency if you are in doubt.

State and Local Works

Keep in mind that the exemption applies only to works of the United States federal government. State and local governments are left to decide whether their own works will have copyright protection. Inquire with the appropriate state agency about possible copyright protection for its materials.

The Idaho legislature has provided a blunt example of a state making a direct declaration about copyright for its statutes: "The Idaho Code is the property of the state of Idaho, and the state of Idaho and the taxpayers shall be deemed to have a copyright on the Idaho Code." Idaho Code Section 9-350 (1997).

Chapters 10 and 11 look at another important way that works may be in the public domain: copyrights expire after some period of years.

Source

Crews, Kenneth D. *Copyright Law and Graduate Research: New Media, New Rights, and Your New Dissertation.* 2d ed. Ann Arbor, MI: Bell & Howell Information and Learning, 2000. Available from <http://www.umi.com/hp/Support/DServices/copyrght/>.

Cool website

O'Mahoney, Benedict. *The Copyright Website.* <http://www.benedict.com/>.

8

Formalities of Copyright: Copyright Notice and Registration

The key point: Under today's copyright law, registering the work with the U.S. Copyright Office and placing a copyright notice on it are no longer required to "get copyright." You "get copyright" today automatically as soon as you create an original work that is "fixed." The absence of formalities today does not place the work in the public domain. Their absence is no longer even a reliable clue about whether a work is protected.①

Generosity and Constraint

You can think of this development in two ways. From the view of an author, you can see that the law is extraordinarily generous. You have copyright protection for your new works even if you never know about copyright. From the view of a person seeking to identify materials that might be in the public domain, you need to assume that almost any work that you may find anywhere is now protected, even if you cannot find any mention of copyright, until you do the research to learn otherwise. That research may be simple or highly complex.

Publications Before 1978

On the other hand, because the formalities of notice and (for all practical purposes) registration were required prior to 1978 (when a new copyright law

① A copyright notice is not reliable or required. Nevertheless, the Digital Millennium Copyright Act (DMCA) creates a new federal offense for the removal under some circumstances of "copyright management information," which is defined to include the copyright notice as well as a wide variety of other identifying information. See chapter 15.

took effect in the U.S.), pre-1978 publications without the formalities entered the public domain.②
Under prior law, the lack of a formal copyright notice—such as the "©" symbol with the year and copyright owner's name—indicated the lack of copyright protection.

Words of Advice

Do not overlook the benefits of formalities for your new works. Placing the copyright notice on your work offers valuable information to the reader. Registering a claim with the U.S. Copyright Office gives you important legal benefits in the unlikely event of a lawsuit.③

The next chapter looks at some important nuances of these issues.

Source

Crews, Kenneth D. *Copyright Law and Graduate Research: New Media, New Rights, and Your New Dissertation.* 2d ed. Ann Arbor, MI: Bell & Howell Information and Learning, 2000. Available from <http://www.umi.com/hp/Support/DServices/copyrght/>.

② Under the terms of the World Trade Organization (WTO) treaty, the United States was required to "restore" copyright protection for many foreign works that had entered the public domain in the U.S. for lack of formalities. American works that entered the public domain for the same reason remain there. See Section 104A of the Copyright Act.

③ One of the legal benefits of timely registration is the ability to collect "statutory damages" in an infringement case. In 1999 Congress raised the dollar amounts for statutory damages to $30,000 per work infringed, and to $150,000 in the event of willful infringement. See chapter 39.

9

More about the Formalities of Copyright

Chapter 8 makes the key point that formalities of registration and notice are no longer required for new works, but were required to secure protection for pre-1978 publications. This chapter gives a bit of important elaboration, and probably raises a few tough questions.

Two general rules can help determine whether a work is protected by copyright.

Works Before 1978

Rule One: If the work was published originally in the U.S. before 1978 without a notice or a timely renewal of the copyright as was once required, it lacks copyright protection. Note that this rule applies only to published works. If the work is unpublished, it is still protected, even without the formalities. Chapter 11 focuses on the special rules for unpublished works. Those rules are critical for historians and anyone working with manuscripts, family photos, completed questionnaires, and the like.

Note, too, that this rule generally applies only to U.S. works; many foreign works do not necessarily need the formalities for protection in either their home country or in the U.S. That wrinkle is a long story. For more information about this "restoration" of foreign copyrights, look at *Highlights of Copyright Amendments Contained in the Uruguay Round Agreements Act (URAA), GATT Circular, Circular 38b* among the various information circulars available on the Copyright Office website (address below).

Under this rule, you may need to search for copyright registrations of a work. Registration records are public, and the Copyright Office will conduct searches for a fee. Computer online searches are also available through some database providers and on the Internet. You can find helpful circulars from the Copyright Office on this subject as well.

Works Created Since January 1, 1978

Rule Two: If the work was first created in or after 1978, the lack of a copyright notice or registration is not conclusive. You should proceed as if the work is protected until you learn otherwise from the author or publisher. Keep detailed records of your findings. As a practical matter, this rule means that almost any work you find today—in your desk, in the library, or on the Internet—is presumed to be protected by copyright.

Therein lies the punch line that bears repeating. Just because the work lacks any mention of copyright does not mean that it is therefore in the public domain.

Copyrights also expire at some point. Chapters 10 and 11 provide explanation of the "duration" of copyright.

For further information

For helpful background about registration, searching records, protection of foreign works, and many other topics, see the U.S. Copyright Office information circulars, available from <http://lcweb.loc.gov/copyright/circs/>.

10

How Long Do Copyrights Last?
The Duration Question

Copyrights do not last forever; protections can lapse, and the work enters the public domain. The U.S. Constitution specifies that copyright shall last only for "limited times." Current law grants privileges in most cases for the life of the author, plus seventy years.① The basic rule for most works had been "life-plus-fifty," but in late 1998 Congress added twenty more years of protection to existing and future copyrights.②

The law protects anonymous and pseudonymous works—and "works made for hire"—for ninety-five years from their first publication, or 120 years from their creation, whichever term expires first.③ An upcoming chapter explains "works made for hire" and their significance for education.

History of Change

Before Congress fully revised copyright law, with a new act that went into effect in 1978, the duration of copyright was considerably different. Under the old law (i.e., before 1978), copyrights for published works lasted for twenty-eight years, plus a renewal for another twenty-eight years. In the early 1960s that renewal term was stretched to forty-seven years, for a total of seventy-five years of protection. As a carryover from those days, and with the recent addition of twenty more years, the rule today for works published before 1978 is that they are generally protected for a maximum of ninety-five

① In October 1998, Congress enacted the Sonny Bono Copyright Term Extension Act, which added 20 years to the term of protection. Public Law No. 105-298, 112 Stat. 2827 (1998).

② A group of publishers that reprint public-domain works challenged the constitutionality of term extension in early 1999, arguing that it violates the "limited times" requirement of copyright. A federal district court rejected the challenge. *Eldred v. Reno*, 74 F. Supp.2d 1 (D.D.C. 1999).

③ Before the Term Extension Act these terms had been 75 and 100 years, respectively.

years. That protection for pre-1978 works still depends on formalities (see chapters 8 and 9) and in many cases on renewal of the copyright with the U.S. Copyright Office.

An Important Twist

What does all of this mean today? It means that as a general rule, if you find a work that was first published more than ninety-five years ago, it is in the public domain. Here is an important twist on that rule. Before Congress added twenty years to copyright protection in 1998, copyrights in works that had been published in 1922 and before already had expired. They remain expired. Those works received at most seventy-five years of protection and are now in the public domain.

Other the other hand, works published in 1923 and before 1978 may now have up to ninety-five years of protection; they will not begin to enter the public domain until the end of 2018. The law here can get even more convoluted, but these basic points will likely meet the needs of most researchers and librarians.

Note that this chapter has been about published works. The special rules for unpublished works will be the subject of the next chapter.

*For further information*④

Cohen, Saul. "Duration." *UCLA Law Review* 24 (1977): 1180-1231.

Crews, Kenneth D. *Copyright Law and Graduate Research: New Media, New Rights, and Your New Dissertation.* 2d ed. Ann Arbor, MI: Bell & Howell Information and Learning, 2000. Available from <http://www.umi.com/hp/Support/DServices/copyrght/> [includes an abbreviated table on the duration issue].

④ For more information about term extension and public domain, see the Copyright Commons website available from <http://cyber.law.harvard.edu/cc/>.

Gasaway, Laura N. *When Works Pass into the Public Domain.* Available from <http://www.unc.edu/~unclng/public-d.htm> [Prof. Gasaway has prepared a most helpful chart to clarify many of the duration issues].

For more information about the contentious debate over copyright term extension

Karjala, Dennis. "Comment of U.S. Copyright Law Professors on the Copyright Office Term of Protection Study." *European Intellectual Property Review* 12 (1994): 531-37. Available from <http://www.public.asu.edu/~dkarjala/legmats/1998Statement.html>.

Opposing Copyright Extension: A Forum for Information on Proposals to Extend the Term of Copyright Protection and What to Do about It. Available from <http://www.public.asu.edu/~dkarjala/index.html>.

11

How Long Do Copyrights Last?
Unpublished Works

Historians, sociologists, and other scholars frequently work with unpublished materials, and special rules of duration apply to these works. Unpublished works might include diaries, letters, survey responses, manuscripts, photographs, art, or software—any type of work that has not been distributed to the public in copies. The basic rule for works created after January 1, 1978, whether published or not, is that copyright lasts for the life of the author plus seventy years.[1]

The End of Common Law

On the other hand, if the work was created before 1978, but never published, a complex set of rules applies. The pre-1978 law granted "common-law" copyright for works that remained unpublished. A manuscript left in the desk drawer had "common-law" privileges, and the statutory privileges began only upon publication. A principal difference between the pre-1978 statutory and common-law regimes was that statutory rights lasted only for the limited period (previously twenty-eight years, plus a possible renewal for twenty-eight years or more), while common-law rights lasted in perpetuity. Perpetuity. Forever.

As long as the manuscript, letter, or other work was never published, the creator's rights never expired. The author might have been dead for centuries, but

[1] In October 1998, Congress enacted the Sonny Bono Copyright Term Extension Act, which added 20 years to the term of protection. The basic term today is life of the author, plus 70 years. Public Law No. 105-298, 112 Stat. 2827 (1998).

24

the copyright lived on. Congress finally brought an end to that situation with passage of the new Copyright Act in 1976. The 1976 Act rescinds all common-law copyright and now subjects the older, unpublished works to a statutory term of protection: generally life plus seventy years.②

The Importance of 2003

To prevent abrupt termination of long-standing copyrights, however, the law provides that none of the former common-law rights will expire until after December 31, 2002. Thus, in 2003 and in each subsequent year, the unpublished works of authors who died seventy years before will enter the public domain.③ Until then, the privileges of copyright and the limits of fair use apply to the manuscripts, letters, and diaries of even America's leading historical figures.

Source

Crews, Kenneth D. *Copyright Law and Graduate Research: New Media, New Rights, and Your New Dissertation.* 2d ed. Ann Arbor, MI: Bell & Howell Information and Learning, 2000. Available from <http://www.umi.com/hp/Support/DServices/copyrght/>.

For further information

Crews, Kenneth D. "Do Your Manuscripts Have a Y2K+3 Problem?" *Library Journal* 125 (June 15, 2000): 38-40.

② Before the Term Extension Act, the protection had been for the life of the author, plus 50 years.

③ While the Term Extension Act did add 20 years to the duration of the copyrights, it did not alter the expiration date of December 31, 2002. In 2003, we can still look forward to unpublished works entering the public domain, although the author must now have been dead for 70 years, not 50 years.

12

Who Owns the Copyright?
The General Rule and Some Exceptions

For each new work that is copyrightable, someone is the copyright owner. The general rule is that the owner of copyright is the person who does the creative work. If you write the book, you own the copyright. If you take the photograph, you own the copyright. If you design the website . . . well, you get the idea. Copyrights may also be owned jointly. More about that in the next chapter.

An important exception to this basic rule is the doctrine of "work made for hire" (WMFH). For these works, the employer of the person who does the creative work is considered the author and the copyright owner. The employer may be a firm, an organization, or an individual.

What Is a WMFH?

The leading type of WMFH is a work prepared by an employee within the scope of his or her employment. In that situation, the copyright belongs to the employer. Another type of WMFH is a work specially ordered or commissioned for use as a contribution to a collective work, part of a motion picture or other audiovisual work, a sound recording, a translation, a supplementary work, a compilation, an instructional text, a test, answer material for a test, or an atlas.[1] Even if the work is within one of these categories, the parties must still expressly agree in a written instrument signed by both parties that the work shall be considered a WMFH.

[1] The Intellectual Property and Communications Omnibus Reform Act of 1999 added "sound recordings" to the list of works that may become "works made for hire" if both parties expressly agree in a written instrument. Public Law No. 106-113, 113 Stat. 1501 (1999).

Examples of possible works made for hire created in an employment relationship are:

- A software program created by a staff programmer for Creative Computer Corporation.
- A newspaper article written by a staff journalist for publication in a daily newspaper.
- A musical arrangement written for XYZ Music Company by a salaried arranger on its staff.
- A sound recording created by the staff engineers of ABC Record Company.

Employee or Contractor

Many of the hard issues surrounding the WMFH doctrine center on whether the project was created in the context of "employment." If you are an employee, your work starts to fit within the rule. But if you are an "independent contractor," you are not an employee at all; the copyrights are likely to stay with you. This result is highly problematic. You may pay a computer programmer a vast fortune, or you may pay a tidy sum for photos of your kids, but paying money does not make the work "for hire." The freelance programmer and the photography studio most likely still hold the copyrights.

Predicaments and Solutions

Colleges and universities often find themselves in this predicament. They pay thousands of dollars for the services of a photographer, a video producer, or a public relations firm, only to discover that the outside company still holds the copyright and can control the use of the material.

There is at least one practical solution to this dilemma: copyrights may be transferred. If the law resolves that the photographer or programmer owns the copyright, but that is not the desired result, the parties may agree to move the ownership to the hiring party. More about that possibility in the following chapters.

By the way, one additional consequence of the WMFH doctrine is that it changes the term of copyright protection. Recall the general rule: works are protected for the life of the author, plus seventy years. In the case of a WMFH, protection lasts for the shorter of either ninety-five years from first publication or 120 years from creation.②

②These terms of protection reflect the addition of 20 years pursuant to the Sonny Bono Copyright Term Extension Act of 1998. See chapter 10.

Source

U.S. Copyright Office. *Works Made for Hire under the 1976 Copyright Act, Circular 9.* Washington, D.C., 2000. Available from <http://lcweb.loc.gov/copyright/circs/circ09.pdf>.

For further information

Kilby, Pamela A. "The Discouragement of Learning: Scholarship Made for Hire." *Journal of College and University Law* 21 (1995): 455-88.

13

Who Owns the Copyright?
Joint Copyright Ownership

Scenario: Professor X and Professor Y create a study aid for their chemistry class. Professor X prepares an updated version of the material for her class. Does Professor X need permission from Professor Y? Is one professor allowed to find a publisher for the "joint work" without permission from the other author?

What Is a Joint Work?

The Copyright Act defines a joint work as "a work prepared by two or more authors with the intention that their contributions be merged into inseparable or interdependent parts of a unitary whole" (Section 101, reprinted at appendix A1 of this book). "Inseparable" contributions might be blended into a co-authored textbook or article. "Interdependent" contributions might be the words and music for one song or the text and images for a multimedia work.[1]

Two Requirements

A joint work generally must meet two requirements. First, each co-author must contribute copyrightable expression to the joint project. If one party gives only an idea for the project, that person has not provided copyrightable expression. Second, each of the parties must have had the intent to create a

[1] A recent case involving the motion picture *Malcolm X* illustrates the sometimes difficult task of determining who is the author of a complex, collaborative effort. In the case of *Aalmuhammed v. Lee,* 202 F.3d 1227 (9th Cir. 2000), the plaintiff assisted the filmmakers to make the movie consistent with Islamic practices. The plaintiff also rewrote several sections of the script to achieve consistency. However, the court found that even if he contributed copyrighted material, he nevertheless was not an "author" of the motion picture. The evidence showed no intent by any party that he would "co-author" the work. Similarly, an editor or colleague who makes substantial suggestions for improving your journal article is also not likely a co-author or joint copyright owner.

joint work at the time the work was created. That intent is not the specific requirement that the parties thought about their work in legal terms. In general, this requirement means that the authors had an intent or expectation that their contributions would be combined into a unified work.

Who Owns a Joint Work?

Each owner holds an undivided share in the copyright. This means that each co-owner can use or license the entire work as he or she wishes, but must account for profits to the other joint owners. On the other hand, each co-owner acting alone cannot transfer the copyright to another party or grant an exclusive right to use the work without the consent of the other co-owners.

In the scenario above, each professor as co-owner may use the work and grant non-exclusive rights of use to others. Each professor may also update the work, at least for his or her own purposes. But each one must remain accountable to the other for the advantages and problems that result from individual decisions. On the other hand, giving exclusive rights, such as to a publisher, usually requires consent by both authors.

Joint ownership is a management headache. Joint owners should attempt to reach an agreement with one another about the future use of the work before they create it.

Copyright protection for a jointly owned work usually lasts throughout the life of the last of the authors to die, plus seventy more years. Some writers have sought youthful co-authors in order to boost the likelihood of prolonging legal rights.

For further information

Versteeg, Russ. "Defining 'Author' for Purposes of Copyright." *American University Law Review* 45 (1996): 1323-66.

14

Who Owns the Copyright?
Exceptions, Assignment, and Institutional Policies

The previous chapters emphasize that the person who does the creative work is generally the owner of the copyright. The work-made-for-hire doctrine is an important exception. Under those basic legal principles, you can determine who is the copyright owner of most works. At least you can determine who was the initial copyright owner. The ownership of copyrights often changes hands. Michael Jackson has purchased controlling rights to numerous Beatles songs. The simple song "Happy Birthday to You" is one of the most valuable copyright-protected works, and those rights have been bought and sold for enormous amounts of money.

Transfer or Assignment

Copyrights can be bought, sold, willed to someone, or simply given away. A transfer of the copyright or an exclusive grant or license to use the work is a transaction that must be in writing, and the writing must be signed by the party making the transfer or granting the exclusive right to use the work. Thus, you could write a song or paint a painting, and you could give away or sell the copyright to those works. To do so, however, you must put the fact of that transaction in writing, and you must sign it.

Transferring the object is distinct from transferring the copyright. For example, you may create a painting and sell it to an appreciative collector. But selling the painting does not include a sale of the copyright unless you specifically agree to include the copyright, and you put the transfer in a signed writing. That result does not change even if you were paid millions of dollars for the art.

Scholarly Publishing Contracts

We experience this rule on a daily basis. We go to the bookstore and buy a book. We have purchased the book, but we have not acquired the copyright. In the academic world, we also routinely transfer our copyrights. A professor writes an article and, as the author, likely owns the copyright to it. Some journal publishers, however, upon accepting the article for publication, require that the author assign the copyright to the publisher by signing a document specifically transferring the copyright.[1] Many of us in academia have published works and assigned the copyrights, but not all journal publishers require assignment of the copyright.[2] Whether the author or the publisher owns the copyright to a particular article is a factual matter that needs to be investigated with each work.

Institutional Policies

Because the "work-made-for-hire" doctrine may leave some lingering questions about whether the copyright in fact belongs to the creator of the work or belongs to the employer, agreements and institutional policies can be helpful to resolve situations. Many employers have policies or employment agreements to clarify who owns the copyright to new works and how the rights of ownership and royalties may be allocated between the creator of the work and the employer.

The tradition at most colleges and universities has been to leave the copyrights with the faculty, and we are not likely to see sweeping changes in that tradition soon. Yet we are seeing careful and meticulous changes in institutional policies that shift some ownership rights in some works to the

[1] This common practice of assigning copyrights to publishers has led to a serious dysfunction in scholarly communications. Publishers that hold all rights have been able to impose escalating fees for subscriptions and permissions, hindering access to research and scholarship. The SPARC project is an ambitious initiative intended to break this cycle by offering more constructive alternatives for scholarly publishing. For more information about SPARC, visit <http://www.arl.org/sparc>.

[2] Authors who are faced with a publication contract that seeks assignment of the copyright should not hesitate to negotiate new terms or at least reserve rights to use his or her own work in future teaching and writing, or find a different publisher. For an example of a negotiated alternative to the standard contract, see the introduction to the following series of articles: Kenneth D. Crews and Dwayne K. Buttler, eds., "Perspectives on Fair-Use Guidelines for Education and Libraries," *Journal of the American Society for Information Science* 51 (December 1999): 1303-57.

institution. The growth of distance education and the considerable financial consequences of creating and marketing new works has stirred the need to reexamine the feasibility of traditional and simplistic concepts of intellectual property at educational institutions.③

Unbundling Rights

The law can only bestow the copyright and all of its privileges on a particular owner. Policies and agreements, however, offer the opportunity to "unbundle" the rights and to share or allocate them more equitably among the interested parties. Policymakers need to look away from the law and toward institutional objectives to find more creative and desirable solutions.

For further information

Ownership of New Works at the University: Unbundling of Rights and the Pursuit of Higher Learning. Seal Beach, CA: Consortium for Educational Technology for University Systems, 1997. Available from <http://www.cetus.org/ownership.pdf>.

Ownership of journal articles is proving to be hotly controversial. See: Bachrach, Steven, et al., "Who Should Own Scientific Papers?" *Science* 281 (September 1998): 1459-60. Available from <http://www.sciencemag.org/cgi/content/full/281/5382/1459>.

Courts have begun to address whether a professor's scholarly article is a "work made for hire." In one case, the professor apparently did not contest the university's claim of rights in order to pursue litigation against a third party. *University of Colorado Foundation v. American Cyanamid*, 880 F. Supp. 1387, *recons. in part*, 902 F. Supp. 221 (D. Colo. 1995), *reh'g denied*, 196 F.3d 1366 (1999), *petition for cert. filed*, 68 U.S.L.W. 3614 (Mar. 16, 2000) (No. 99-1526). Ownership of the copyrights was not an issue during the appeals.④

③ For an excellent website on the issue of ownership of faculty works, with links to numerous university policies see: Rodney J. Petersen, *Copyown: A Resource on Copyright Ownership for the Higher Education Community,* available from <http://www.inform.umd.edu/CompRes/NEThics/copyown/>.

④ In a more recent case, a court ruled with little analysis that a professor's instructional materials are WMFH and belong to the college. *Vanderhurst v. Colorado Mountain College Dist.*, 16 F. Supp.2d 1297 (D. Colo. 1998).

15

The Expanding Rights of Copyright Owners

The copyright owner of a work has specific "exclusive rights" in that work. In this context "exclusive" means that the copyright owner may exercise those rights and other individuals may not. For example, owners hold the right to make copies of the work. If someone else makes a copy, it can be an infringement (unless it is fair use). The fundamental statutory rights of the copyright owner are as follows:

- The right to reproduce the work in copies.
- The right to distribute the work publicly.
- The right to make derivative works.
- The right of public display of the work.
- The right of public performance of that work.
- The right of public performance of sound recordings "by means of a digital audio transmission."[1]

[1] In 1995 Congress added this sixth provision. Digital Performance Right in Sound Recordings Act of 1995, Public Law No. 104-39, 109 Stat. 336 (1995).

The next few chapters in this book elaborate on the meaning of these rights.

Moral Rights

A relatively recent addition to owners' rights is the concept of "moral rights." Moral rights apply only to a narrow class of works. In 1990 Congress amended the Copyright Act by granting "moral rights" with respect to certain "works of visual arts." Moral rights in general apply only to original works of art, sculpture, and other works of visual arts that are produced in 200 copies or fewer. For example, moral rights may apply to a limited series lithograph, but likely do not apply to a photograph used in a mass-market magazine.②

Moral rights grant to the artist the right to have his or her name kept on the work or to have the artist's name removed from it if the work has been altered in a way objectionable to the artist. Moral rights also give artists limited abilities to prevent their works from being defaced or destroyed.

A leading case on the issue of moral rights awarded monetary damages to an artist whose work was intentionally destroyed. The federal district court ruled that the city of Indianapolis violated the moral rights of a sculptor when the city demolished his large, metal work that had been installed on city property.③

Digital Audio Transmissions

Sound recordings were first given federal copyright protection in 1972, but without public performance rights. When a radio station plays a new song on the air, the composer has a performance right and receives a royalty. The performers who made the recording do not have performance rights and are entitled to no payment. The performers, however, do get money from sales of recordings, because the copyright in the recording does include rights of reproduction and distribution.

The development of the Internet as a medium for delivering music has threatened to cut into the sales of recordings. If a user can receive transmitted performances of selected recordings on demand, the user has little need to buy CDs. To protect the interests of copyright owners of the recordings, in 1995 Congress granted performances rights, but only in the context of "digital audio performances." The statute is enormously complex and runs for pages of convoluted conditions and exceptions.④

② For the statute on moral rights, see Section 106A of the Copyright Act; be sure as well to read the definition of "works of visual arts" in Section 101, reprinted at appendix A1.

③ *Martin v. Indianapolis*, 982 F. Supp. 625 (S.D. Ind. 1997), *aff'd*, 192 F.3d 608 (7th Cir. 1999).

④ See Section 114(d) of the Copyright Act.

In general, an "interactive" digital system—including a website—that delivers recordings on demand may now implicate rights of both the composer and the performer.

Technological Protection Systems

The Digital Millennium Copyright Act of 1998 (DMCA) added new rights for copyright owners. The first allows owners to use password protections and other technological measures to control access to copyrighted works. Circumventing those measures to gain access without permission can now be a federal violation.[5]

This statute is also filled with exceptions.[6] One exception allows nonprofit libraries to circumvent protection systems in order to access a work for purposes of evaluating it to determine whether to acquire a copy of the work for a use that is lawful under the Copyright Act. As if that point were not sufficiently obscure, this exception is further loaded with limits and conditions. Moreover, if the library applies it incorrectly and makes unlawful access, monetary penalties can be significant. Fortunately, nonprofit libraries, archives, and educational institutions are exempt from the criminal sanctions that apply to everyone else. One has to wonder if this exception, carefully crafted for libraries, will be of much practical use. At best, it might be a bargaining chip to get permission to "sample" a database before making a costly purchase.

Other exceptions can allow reverse engineering of software and research on encryption techniques. These exceptions also apply only under constrained circumstances and only subject to numerous conditions. Quite simply, do not try this law at home. You need professional guidance.

[5] See Section 1201 of the Copyright Act.

[6] Yet another set of exceptions may be forthcoming under the authority of the Librarian of Congress, with advice from the U.S. Copyright Office, to exempt a specified "class of copyrighted works" from the anti-circumvention prohibitions. The Copyright Office is as of this writing holding hearings and preparing to draft regulatory exemptions. For more information, see <http://www.loc.gov/copyright/1201/anticirc.html>.

Copyright Management Information

The DMCA also includes protection for "copyright management information" (CMI) that may be associated with works.[7] CMI is broadly defined to include not only a copyright notice, but also the name of the author or copyright owner, the title of the work, and the performers and writers credited on an audiovisual work. CMI also encompasses terms and conditions for use of the work—such as restrictive prohibitions printed in a book and "click-on" contracts governing downloaded materials.

This law creates a violation, for example, when one intentionally removes or alters CMI in connection with inducing or enabling an infringement of the work. A violation can occur under several other fact patterns, but a violation generally requires an intentional action or at least knowledge that the CMI has been removed or altered. While a violation of this law might therefore be difficult to prove, as a practical matter it nevertheless signals great caution about removing any CMI from a work.

Compare this concept to moral rights. Moral rights in the U.S. apply only to certain works of art and allow the artist to keep his or her name on a work during the life of the artist. The new law about CMI applies to all types of works, protects much more than one's name, and applies apparently throughout the term of copyright protection for the work.

[7] See Section 1202 of the Copyright Act.

16

Rights of the Copyright Owner: Reproduction and Distribution

The right of reproduction of a work means just what it says. Reproducing a work occurs in many circumstances and by means of a vast range of technological tools. We reproduce works when we photocopy pages from a text, when we quote a sentence into a new article, and even when we take verbatim notes from research materials. We reproduce works when we make a transparency of a cartoon to show in class, when we make a videotape that captures images of paintings on the wall, and when we make digital images of works for our websites or multimedia works. We even reproduce works when we print or download a document found on the Web.①

Distribution of works is also surprisingly common. We raise the possibility of distributing copyrighted works when we hand out photocopies in class, make documents available on our website, or even allow people to borrow books from our personal or library collections.②

Many of our daily activities raise the possibility of copyright infringements, but do not forget about the many important exceptions to the rights of the copyright owner. Upcoming chapters examine how "fair use" and other exceptions may rescue many of these possible infringements and make them perfectly lawful. But only within limits.

A few words of advance warning are in order. We will discover that the law rarely delineates with great

① A case of considerable importance concluded that one makes a copy of computer software when it is loaded into random-access memory (RAM) of a computer. *MAI Sys. Corp. v. Peak Computer, Inc.*, 991 F.2d 511 (9th Cir. 1993). The DMCA, examined more fully in appendix B, may eliminate potential liability of "online service providers" in a networked environment for RAM copying, caching, and other "automatic" computer operations. See chapter 38.

② A thoroughly disturbing and little-noticed case has held that a library "distributes" works in violation of copyright law when it allows researchers to use materials in the library collection, even if the materials cannot be removed from the premises. This case opens the possibility that a library could be liable for infringement if it has infringing materials in its collections; most libraries could easily and unwittingly have books and other collections that include infringements. *Hotaling v. Church of Jesus Christ of Latter-Day Saints*, 118 F.3d 199 (4th Cir. 1997).

clarity the distinction between infringement and fair use. We will also see that fair use does not cover everything that you might expect.

Excellent, practical copyright site

University of Texas Copyright Crash Course. Available from <http://www.utsystem.edu/ogc/ intellectualproperty/cprtindx.htm>.

For more information

Ginsburg, Jane C. "Reproduction of Protected Works for University Research or Teaching." *Journal of the Copyright Society of the U.S.A.* 39 (1992): 181-223.

17

Rights of the Copyright Owner: Derivative Works

Of all of the rights of the copyright owner, the right to make derivative works may be the most difficult to explain, even though examples of derivative works are common. A major example of a derivative work is a motion picture made from a novel. An author writes the novel and owns the copyright to it. The motion picture studio needs to secure permission from the novelist before preparing a screenplay and shooting the film.

Do not give up on the possibility that someone may pay you big bucks to make a movie from your scholarly work. More realistically, however, we deal with possible derivative works in situations such as these: a digitized version of an analog recording, image, or text; the making of a teacher's manual and other works to support an existing textbook; the creation of artwork from or inspired by an existing picture or image; the production of a new ballet or play from any existing story.① The Happy Meal at McDonald's often includes a toy based on a character from a Disney movie. The toy is a derivative work.

The list of other possible derivative works is nearly endless:

- An index to a book
- A sound recording of a musical composition
- An abridgment of a novel
- A translation

① A digital version of a photograph showing a cityscape, significantly altered, is a derivative work. *Tiffany Design, Inc. v. Reno-Tahoe Specialty, Inc.*, 55 F. Supp.2d 1113 (D. Nev. 1999).

Recall this statement from chapter 4: "Homer's epic poems may never have had any legal protection in their first incarnation, but a new translation is an 'original' work subject to new copyright protection." A new translation is a new derivative work. As a new "original" work, it is also entitled to copyright protection. But be careful: A derivative work made without permission of the owner of the original work (if still under copyright) can be an infringement and may not be entitled to legal protection.

For further information

Goldstein, Paul. "Derivative Rights and Derivative Works in Copyright." *Journal of the Copyright Society of U.S.A.* 30 (February 1983): 209-52.

A helpful source

Strong, William S. *The Copyright Book: A Practical Guide*. 5th ed. Cambridge: MIT Press, 1999.

18

Rights of the Copyright Owner:
Public Performance and Display

Performances and displays are common occurrences in higher education. A "display" can be the simple showing of a page of text or a picture to any viewer. A work is performed when the text is read aloud, the lines of a play are read or acted, a videotape or a film is shown on a screen or monitor, or a song is played or sung aloud. The performance or display can become a possible infringement only when it is "public." A "public" performance or display occurs, among other circumstances, when it is made to a substantial number of persons beyond the usual circle of friends, family, and social acquaintances.[1]

[1] See the definition of "To perform or display a work 'publicly'" in Section 101 of the Copyright Act, reprinted at appendix A1.

Finding the Hitch

We make public displays and performances of works all the time—even when a museum hangs copyright protected paintings on the walls. You can reasonably reach only one conclusion at this point: What is the hitch? Why are museums still in business?

Here is the hitch: Important exemptions blow big holes in these rights of the copyright owner. For example, a specific exemption allows the owner of a lawfully made copy of the work, such as a painting, a poster, or a photograph, to display that work where it is located. Thus, the museum can hang art on the walls, you can put posters in the classroom, the library can put books and their contents in display cases, and we can project slides onto a screen.[2]

[2] See Section 109(c) of the Copyright Act.

No similar exemption, however, applies to performances. Consequently, no broad exemption covers the prospect of showing a movie in an auditorium or acting out a play on a school stage.

Classroom Teaching

On the other hand, the really important and good news is that the law does permit displays and performances in the context of the "face-to-face" classroom. Therefore, when we are teaching our classes in front of a group of students, we can read the text, recite the poetry, play the video, sing the songs, and even show those slides. The whole situation changes, however, when we switch from the "face-to-face" classroom and begin to transmit the materials in distance learning.[3]

For further information

For a bit more about displays and performances in the classroom and about the complexities of distance learning, see:

Crews, Kenneth D. *Copyright and Distance Education: Lawful Uses of Protected Works.* Indianapolis: Indiana Higher Education Telecommunication System, 1995. Available from <http://www.ihets.org/distance_ed/ipse/fdhandbook/copyrt.html>.

An updated and revised version of that paper appears as an essay at pp. 377-94 in:

Gasaway, Laura N., ed. *Growing Pains: Adapting Copyright for Libraries, Education, and Society.* Littleton, CO: Fred B. Rothman & Co., 1997.

[3] See Section 110(1) and 110(2) of the Copyright Act, reprinted in appendix A6. The U.S. Copyright Office in May 1999 issued a major report on the subject of displays and performances in distance education. See chapter 31 and appendix C.

19

Exceptions to the Rights of Owners

This book so far has followed the basic structure of copyright law: the law grants a broad set of rights to a broad range of materials, then it proceeds to carve out exceptions to those rights. The next several chapters take a close look at the best known of those exceptions, fair use. Yet, the U.S. Copyright Act includes not fewer than fifteen statutory provisions that establish exceptions to the rights of the copyright owner. In effect, those exceptions allow to the public the right to make certain specified uses of the copyrighted works of others. Many of those exceptions are of direct importance to academic work and librarianship. Here are a few of those important exceptions, with references to their section numbers in the U.S. Copyright Act:

Section 107: Fair Use. This provision may be thought of as the "umbrella" exception that is broad and flexible in its application to an unlimited variety of unpredictable situations where someone may make uses of copyrighted works, ranging from simple quotations in a new article to complex cutting and pasting of pieces of works into a new collage, multimedia work, or website. The following chapters explore the meaning and limits of fair use.

Section 108: Library Copying. Upcoming chapters also examine this provision in some detail. Unlike the flexibility and general nature of fair use, this statute and most of the other statutory exceptions are highly detailed in their application. Section 108 provides that most academic and public libraries, as well as many other libraries, may make copies of certain types of works for specific purposes.①

Section 109(a): The First-Sale Doctrine. This important exception limits the "distribution right" of the copyright holder by providing that once the owner authorizes the release of lawfully made copies of a work, those copies may in turn be passed along to others by sale, rental, loan, gift, or other transfer. Without this important exception, a bookstore could not sell you a book, the library could not let you check out a book, the video store could not rent a movie, and you could not give books, CDs, and videos to your friends as birthday presents. Without this exception, all of those transactions might be unlawful distributions. You can begin to see that the exceptions often make daily activity feasible.

Section 109(c): Exception for Public Displays. This provision limits the "public display right" of the copyright owner by allowing the owner of a lawfully made copy of a work to display it to the public at the place where that work is located. Thus, the art museum that owns a painting may hang it on the wall and let the public enter the front door to view it. The bookstore can place books on display in front windows. The library may put its rare and valuable works in the display cases for all to see. Without this exception, those activities could be infringements.

Section 110(1): Displays and Performances in Face-to-Face Teaching. Chapter 18 notes that this exception is valuable for reciting poetry, reading plays, showing videos, playing music, and engaging in many other performances and displays of protected works in the traditional classroom setting.

Section 110(2): Displays and Performances in Distance Learning. Once we turn on the cameras and transmit the classroom experience through distance learning, the law makes an abrupt shift. The law here is not pleasant.② Chapter 31 provides details.

① The Digital Millennium Copyright Act of 1998 amends Section 108 to clarify when libraries may use digital technology to preserve works in the collection and to reproduce works when the technological format has become obsolete. More details in chapter 33.

② The law could become more pleasant. In the DMCA, Congress directed the U.S. Copyright Office to study copyright and distance education. Chapter 31 and appendix C summarize the report and the recommendations from the Copyright Office.

Section 117: Computer Software. This provision generally allows the owner of a copy of a computer program to modify the program to work on his or her computer or computer platform, and to make a back-up copy of the software to use in the event of damage to or destruction of the original copy.③

Section 120: Architectural Works. Architectural designs are protected by copyright, limiting your ability to copy the design from one building into another. But Section 120 makes clear that once the building is constructed at a place visible to the public, anyone may make and use a picture of that building without infringing the copyright. Architectural historians and structural engineers can be spared from infringement when they take pictures of existing structures and use them in teaching and research. Moreover, the photograph itself is a new copyrighted work apart from the copyright in the architectural design.

Section 121: Special Formats for Persons Who Are Blind or Have Other Disabilities. Congress added this provision in 1996 to allow certain types of organizations to make specific types of formats of published, nondramatic literary works in order that they may be useful to persons who are blind or have other disabilities.

These exceptions share one enormously important common characteristic. They apply only if your situation has met all of the required conditions specified in the statute. Please do not rely on this brief summary as the foundation for your decision to use copyrighted works.

For further information

For the full text of these statutes, take a look at the U.S. Copyright Act available from <http://lcweb.loc.gov/copyright/title17/>.

For a seriously dated but helpful overview of some of these exceptions, see: Leon E. Seltzer, *Exemptions and Fair Use in Copyright* (Cambridge: Harvard University Press, 1978).

③The DMCA also brought changes in Section 117 to clarify that computer software may be reproduced in order to repair the computer on which the program is originally loaded. This change is in direct response to the *MAI* case noted in chapter 5.

The Rock-and-Roll Case

Of related interest is a court decision that prohibited a photographer from selling photographs that he took of the Rock and Roll Hall of Fame Museum in Cleveland, Ohio. The court originally held that the commercial exploitation was an infringement of the museum's trademark rights in the design of its building. The court did not rule that the photograph was an infringement of any copyright. Although the trademark decision was reversed on appeal, it still suggests that we might clear the copyright problems with respect to a project, and still be left with other legal issues to resolve. For the full text of the museum decision, see: *Rock and Roll Hall of Fame and Museum, Inc. v. Gentile Productions*, 134 F.3d 749 (6th Cir. 1998).

20

Fair Use:
What Exactly Is It?

Fair use is both an opportunity and a source of confusion. Fair use is an essential balance to the wide range of rights that copyright law grants to copyright owners. Recall that even simple quoting can constitute an unlawful "reproduction" of the original work. Yet often it is not unlawful; fair use can rescue many infringements and turn them into proper uses—but only within limits.

No Established Answers

Nearly everyone will disagree on what is "fair," and no one has a definitive, legally binding "answer" to most fair-use questions. Congress deliberately created a flexible fair-use statute that gives no exact parameters. Fair use depends on the circumstances of each case.

The law offers four factors to evaluate and to balance in any determination of fair use:

1. The purpose of the use, including a nonprofit educational purpose;
2. The nature of the copyrighted work;
3. The amount of the copying; and
4. The effect of the copying on the potential market for, or value of, the original work.

In applying these factors, many of us might agree that most short quotations from published works in a scholarly publication are fair use. On the other hand, the greater the excerpt quoted, for example, the less likely it will be "fair." These examples are relatively easy to grasp, but difficult questions surround more complex cases involving innovative uses of distinctive materials, such as standardized survey instruments, videotapes, or computer software.[1]

Endless Possibilities

Possible "fair use" examples are innumerable. Many uses require a fresh application of the four factors, and they may never produce easy or absolute answers. Courts also have provided little guidance for most educational needs. The fair use of materials in scholarly endeavors is rarely the subject of judicial decisions; the litigation costs and attorney fees are prohibitive. Yet courts are not insensitive to academic needs, and the statute acknowledges the importance of educational uses. Some rulings have recognized that the growth of scholarship depends on using previous works, particularly in writing biographies or history.

The following chapters detail the meaning of the four factors and summarize a few court cases that demonstrate what the factors mean when applied to situations relevant to education.

Source

Crews, Kenneth D. *Copyright Law and Graduate Research: New Media, New Rights, and Your New Dissertation.* 2d ed. Ann Arbor, MI: Bell & Howell Information and Learning, 2000. Available from <http://www.umi.com/hp/Support/DServices/copyrght/>.

For further information

Crews, Kenneth D. *Copyright, Fair Use, and the Challenges for Universities: Promoting the Progress of Higher Education.* Chicago: University of Chicago Press, 1993.

[1] In *Higgins v. Detroit Educational Broadcasting Foundation*, 4 F. Supp.2d 701 (E.D. Mich. 1998), the court allowed as fair use the incorporation of short excerpts of a musical work into the background of a production that was broadcast on a local PBS affiliate and sold in limited copies to educational institutions. Chapter 24 provides more details about this case.

21

Learning about Fair Use: Start with the Statute

Fair use is the subject of numerous misconceptions and myths. The best place to begin a clear understanding of fair use is the statute itself. You might be surprised to learn that the fair-use statute takes only a minute to read, and it is an act of Congress in simple, clear language. The statute is the real source of fair-use law in the United States.

United States Code, Title 17, Section 107

Notwithstanding the provisions of sections 106 and 106A, the fair use of a copyrighted work, including such use by reproduction in copies or phonorecords or by any other means specified in that section,① for purposes such as criticism, comment, news reporting, teaching (including multiple copies for classroom use), scholarship, or research, is not an infringement of copyright. In determining whether the use made of a work in any particular case is a fair use the factors to be considered shall include—

(1) the purpose and character of the use, including whether such use is of a commercial nature or is for nonprofit educational purposes;

(2) the nature of the copyrighted work;

① An early draft of the Digital Millennium Copyright Act contained a provision to delete this clause of Section 107. That provision ultimately was dropped from the bill and is not included in the DMCA as enacted by Congress.

(3) the amount and substantiality of the portion used in relation to the copyrighted work as a whole; and

(4) the effect of the use upon the potential market for or value of the copyrighted work.

The fact that a work is unpublished shall not itself bar a finding of fair use if such finding is made upon consideration of all the above factors.

That is it. That is the statute on fair use. That statute gives the framework for answering the extensive variety of questions you might have about clipping materials for websites, quoting from articles, making handouts for teaching, or sampling other recordings in a rap-music recording. Numerous court cases then apply that framework to the facts at issue in order to determine whether the activity is fair use or infringement.

Is Your Project Within "Fair Use"?

If you conclude that the work you intend to use in your project is protected by copyright law, you must then assess whether your proposed use is "fair" based on the four factors in the statute. If it is not within fair use, you generally must seek permission from the copyright owner, a process to be described in a later chapter. Consider again the four factors of fair use and their possible application to your needs. Keep in mind that all four factors—and other possible circumstances—work together in the fair-use equation.

Be careful not to reach hasty conclusions, such as assuming that all academic uses are "fair" or that all commercial uses are not fair use. You also need not satisfy all four factors; courts balance them to identify their overall leaning—in favor of or against fair use. The following chapters explain how the four factors might work in common situations.

Chapter 19 summarizes other lawful rights to use materials beyond "fair use." Aside from the flexibility and generality of fair use, the Copyright Act includes specific provisions for the use of materials in the classroom, in distance learning, in libraries, and under other circumstances. Other chapters of this book survey a few of those statutes.

Source

Crews, Kenneth D. *Copyright Law and Graduate Research: New Media, New Rights, and Your New Dissertation*. 2d ed. Ann Arbor, MI: Bell & Howell Information and Learning, 2000. Available from <http://www.umi.com/hp/Support/DServices/copyrght/>.

For further information

Consortium for Educational Technology in University Systems (CETUS). *Fair Use of Copyrighted Works: A Crucial Element in Educating America*. Seal Beach, CA: California State Univ. Chancellor's Office, 1995 [joint project of California State University, State University of New York, and City University of New York; Kenneth D. Crews, consultant and author of much of the text]. Available from <http://www.cetus.org/fairindex.html>.

Stanford University Libraries. *Copyright & Fair Use*. Available from <http://fairuse.stanford.edu/>.

22

The First Two Factors of Fair Use: Purpose of the Use and Nature of the Copyrighted Work

Recall from the copyright statute (chapter 21) that the determination of fair use depends on an application of four factors. What do those factors mean? The following is a brief summary.

The Purpose and Character of the Use

Congress explicitly favored nonprofit, educational uses over commercial uses. Copies used in education, but made or sold at monetary profit, may not be so strongly favored. Courts also favor uses that are "transformative" or that are not mere reproductions; fair use is more likely when the copyrighted work is "transformed" into something new or of new utility. Examples might be quotations incorporated into a paper, or perhaps pieces of a work mixed into a multimedia product for your own teaching needs or included in commentary or criticism of the original.①

For teaching purposes, however, multiple copies of some works are specifically allowed, even if not "transformative." The Supreme Court, in a recent decision, mentioned that possibility by focusing on these key words in the statute: "including multiple copies for classroom use." Be careful! This law does not mean that copies for classroom handouts are therefore fair use—you still need to apply in the balance three more factors.

> ① One court found that a "thumbnail" image of a copyrighted photograph could constitute a "transformative" use. *Kelly v. Arriba Soft Corp.*, 77 F. Supp.2d 1116 (C.D. Cal. 1999). A "search engine," ditto.com, used an automated "crawler" to scour the Web for visual images and to index those images in thumbnail form on its website. Users could view thumbnail images generated by the search engine. A photographer claimed that some of the "thumbnail" images infringed his copyrights in photographs from his website. The court held that the resulting "thumbnail" image of a copyrighted photograph "is very different from the use for which the images were originally created." The thumbnail reflected a "transformative" use of the larger image.

The Nature of the Copyrighted Work

This factor examines characteristics of the work being used. What are the qualities or attributes of the book you are copying or the software you are downloading? Many characteristics of a work can affect the application of fair use. For example, several court decisions have concluded that the unpublished "nature" of historical correspondence can weigh against fair use. The court reasoned that copyright owners should have the right to determine the circumstances of "first publication." The authorities are split, however, on whether a published work that is currently out of print should receive special treatment. (Notice that "out of print" is not the same as "no longer under copyright.")

Courts more readily favor the fair use of nonfiction rather than fiction or other "more creative" works. A creative audiovisual work or software program may generally be less appropriate for fair use than might a published sociology text. A consumable workbook will most certainly be subject to less fair use than will a scholarly article.

The next chapter summarizes the other two factors.

Source

Consortium for Educational Technology in University Systems (CETUS). *Fair Use of Copyrighted Works: A Crucial Element in Educating America.* Seal Beach, CA: California State Univ. Chancellor's Office, 1995 [joint project of California State University, State University of New York, and City University of New York; Kenneth D. Crews, consultant and author of much of the text]. Available from <http://www.cetus.org/fairindex.html>.

For further information

American Library Association. *Fair Use in the Electronic Age: Serving the Public Interest* (1995). Available from <http://www.ifla.org/documents/infopol/copyright/fairuse.txt>.

23

The Factors of Fair Use:
Amount of the Work Used and Effect on the Market

The previous chapter summarizes the meaning of the first two factors. The following is an overview of the next two factors.

The Amount and Substantiality of the Portion Used

Amount is measured both quantitatively and qualitatively. No exact measures of allowable quantity exist in the law. Rules about word counts and percentages have no place in the law of fair use. At best, they are interpretations intended to streamline fair use. Quantity must be evaluated relative to the length of the entire original and the amount needed to serve a proper objective. Amount must also be viewed in light of the "nature" of the work being used.

Some works are appropriate for greater uses. One court has ruled that a journal article alone is an entire work, and copying of an entire work at least in a commercial setting usually weighs heavily against fair use.① Pictures generate serious controversies regarding this factor, because a user nearly always wants the full image or the entire "amount."②

Motion pictures are also problematic because even short clips may borrow the most extraordinary or creative elements. One may also reproduce only a small portion of any work but still take "the heart of

① See the *Texaco* decision summarized in chapter 26. On the other hand, when a company copied an entire software program made for a Sony Playstation in order to reverse engineer it and create an emulator, the court ruled that the "amount" factor weighed only slightly against fair use because the Sony program never became part of the new emulator. *Sony Computer Entertainment, Inc. v. Connectix Corp.*, 203 F.3d 596 (9th Cir. 2000).

② One court cautioned that even fleeting images of artistic works in a television production might not tip the "amount" factor sufficiently to outweigh other factors. *Ringgold v. Black Entertainment Television, Inc.*, 126 F.3d 70 (2d Cir. 1997). However, the *Kelly* case mentioned in chapter 22 noted that a low-resolution "thumbnail" image might be important for swaying the "amount" and "effect" factors toward fair use.

the work." The "substantiality" concept represents such a qualitative measure that may weigh against fair use.

So where is the good news for fair use in the "amount" factor? Shorter excerpts from works are more likely to be fair than are longer pieces. Also, keep the amount consistent with the educational or research purpose you may have identified with respect to the first factor. Bear in mind that even if you are copying the "whole article" or digitizing the crucial chariot race from *Ben Hur* (perhaps the "heart" of the film), this factor is only one of four factors: these uses may still not be a problem if the portion is central to your educational purpose, and if the specific material is not realistically marketed for your needs.

The Effect of the Use on the Market or Value

Effect on the market is perhaps even more complicated than the other three factors. Some courts have called it the most important factor, although such statements are often difficult to validate. This factor fundamentally means that if you make a use for which a purchase of an original theoretically should have occurred—regardless of your personal willingness or ability to pay for such purchase—then this factor may weigh against fair use. Occasional quotations or photocopies may have no significant adverse market effect, but reproductions of software and videotapes can make direct inroads on the potential market for those works.

The "effect" factor is closely linked to your "purpose." If your purpose is research or scholarship, market harm may be difficult to prove. If your purpose is commercial, then effect is presumed. More works, however, are being marketed for the academic community, leading to arguments that even educational uses have direct, adverse market consequences.

The next few chapters demonstrate how courts have applied these factors in actual decisions.

Source

Consortium for Educational Technology in University Systems (CETUS). *Fair Use of Copyrighted Works: A Crucial Element in Educating America*. Seal Beach, CA: California State Univ. Chancellor's Office, 1995 [joint project of California State University, State University of New York, and City University of New York; Kenneth D. Crews, consultant and author of much of the text]. Available from <http://www.cetus.org/fairindex.html>.

For further information

International Publishers Copyright Council. *Libraries, Copyright and the Electronic Environment* (1996). Available from <http://www.ifla.org/documents/infopol/copyright/ipa.txt>.

Lawrence, John Shelton and Bernard Timberg. *Fair Use and Free Inquiry: Copyright Law and the New Media*. 2d ed. Norwood, NJ: Ablex Publishing Corp., 1989.

24

Fair Use in the Courts: Quoting from Copyrighted Works

Fair-use cases involving educational activities rarely get to the courts. Numerous colleges and universities have received or sent letters making claims of copyright infringement, but the situations almost never become lawsuits, and lawsuits that result in court decisions involving fair use for education are nearly nonexistent. Consequently, we need to infer what we can from the few cases that have some relevance or analogous applications. This chapter summarizes significant cases about the fair use of quoting or reprinting material from an existing work into a new publication.①

Penelope v. Brown ②

A professor, Penelope, wrote a book about English grammar and language usage. Brown, a writer of popular fiction, later wrote a manual for budding authors. Amidst five pages of Brown's 218-page book, she apparently copied sentence examples from Penelope's work. The court ruled that the use was fair after applying the four factors.

Purpose: The court found that the second book greatly expanded on pieces borrowed from the first, making the use "productive." The court also found little commercial character in the use of the small excerpts, and it found no improper conduct by Brown.

①Courts are slowly beginning to address the fair use of diverse media. In *Higgins v. Detroit Educational Broadcasting Foundation*, 4 F. Supp.2d 701 (E.D. Mich. 1998), the court allowed as fair use the incorporation of short pieces of a musical work into the background of a video production that was broadcast on a local PBS affiliate and sold in limited copies to educational institutions. The court sympathized with the educational and public-service "purpose" of the production. The defendant used a brief "amount"—only about 35 seconds of a popular song— and only in the background of the opening scenes. A song is generally a creative work, so that "nature" tipped in favor of stronger protection and against fair use. The song was not actively licensed for such uses, so the use had no adverse "market effect." Three of the four factors weighed in favor of fair use, and the court ruled accordingly.

② *Penelope v. Brown*, 792 F. Supp. 132 (D. Mass. 1992).

Nature: The court looked to the nonfiction "nature" of the work used and its limited availability to the public.

Amount: The excerpts were a small "amount" of the first work.

Effect: The court found little adverse "effect" on the market for the original, noting that the two books might appear side-by-side in a store, but a buyer is not likely to see one as a replacement for the other.

This case stands for the premise that small excerpts, used to build constructively on the existing work, can often pass fair-use scrutiny.

Maxtone-Graham v. Burtchaell [3]

[3] *Maxtone-Graham v. Burtchaell,* 803 F.2d 1253 (2d Cir. 1986), *cert. denied,* 481 U.S. 1059 (1987).

In 1973, the plaintiff wrote a book based on interviews with women about their own pregnancies and abortions. The defendant wrote his own book on the same subject and sought permission to use lengthy excerpts from the plaintiff's work. The plaintiff refused permission, and the defendant proceeded to publish his work with the unpermitted excerpts.

Purpose: Although defendant's book was published by a commercial press with the possibility of monetary success, the main purpose of the book was to educate the public about abortion and to present the author's views.

Nature: The interviews were largely factual, and fair use applies more broadly to nonfiction.

Amount: Quoting 4.3 percent of the plaintiff's work was not excessive, and the verbatim passages were not necessarily central to the plaintiff's work.

Effect: The court noted that the plaintiff's work was out of print and not likely to appeal to the same readers; the two books appealed to opposing views of the abortion controversy.

This case affirms that quotations in a subsequent work are clearly permissible, sometimes even when they are lengthy. Implicit throughout the case is the fact that the plaintiff was unwilling to allow limited quotations in a book that argued an opposing view of abortion; thus, fair use became the only effective means for the second author to build meaningfully on the scholarly works of others.

Sources

Consortium for Educational Technology in University Systems (CETUS). *Fair Use of Copyrighted Works: A Crucial Element in Educating America*. Seal Beach, CA: California State Univ. Chancellor's Office, 1995 [joint project of California State University, State University of New York, and City University of New York; Kenneth D. Crews, consultant and author of much of the text]. Available from <http://www.cetus.org/fairindex.html>.

Crews, Kenneth D. *Copyright Law and Graduate Research: New Media, New Rights, and Your New Dissertation*. 2d ed. Ann Arbor, MI: Bell & Howell Information and Learning, 2000. Available from <http://www.umi.com/hp/Support/DServices/copyrght/>.

For further information

Bielefeld, Arlene and Lawrence Cheeseman. *Libraries & Copyright Law*. New York: Neal-Schuman Publishers, Inc., 1993.

Stanford University Libraries. *Copyright and Fair Use*. Available from <http://fairuse.stanford.edu>.

25

Fair Use in the Courts: Photocopying for Education

American courts have yet to rule on the question of fair use as applied to photocopying for educational uses. The two cases below are actually about commercial photocopying, although the copies were made to serve student needs.

Basic Books, Inc. v. Kinko's Graphics ①

Kinko's was held to be infringing copyrights when it photocopied book chapters for sale to students as "coursepacks" for their university classes.

Purpose: When conducted by Kinko's, the copying was for commercial purposes and not for educational purposes. The court left open the possibility that the "purpose" may weigh in favor of fair use if the copying were done within the college or university.

Nature: Most of the works were factual—history, sociology, and other fields of study—a factor which weighed in favor of fair use.

Amount: The court analyzed the percentage of each work, finding that five to twenty-five percent of each of the original full books was excessive.

Effect: The court found a direct effect on the market for the books; the coursepacks competed directly with the potential sales of the original books as assigned reading for the students.

① *Basic Books, Inc. v. Kinko's Graphics Corp.*, 758 F. Supp. 1522 (S.D.N.Y. 1991).

Three of the four factors leaned against fair use. The court specifically refused to rule that all coursepacks are infringements, requiring instead that each item in the "anthology" be subject individually to fair-use scrutiny.

Princeton University Press v. Michigan Document Services, Inc. ②

A similar case involving similar facts resulted in a similar decision from the Sixth Circuit Court of Appeals in 1996. That case, known as the *MDS* case, received wide attention in educators' circles when the court at one stage ruled that the copying was fair use. That ruling has since been vacated, and a contrary decision is now the law in that case.③

Source

Consortium for Educational Technology in University Systems (CETUS). *Fair Use of Copyrighted Works: A Crucial Element in Educating America*. Seal Beach, CA: California State Univ. Chancellor's Office, 1995 [joint project of California State University, State University of New York, and City University of New York; Kenneth D. Crews, consultant and author of much of the text]. Available from <http://www.cetus.org/fairindex.html>.

For further information

Crews, Kenneth D. *Not the "Last Word" on Photocopying and Coursepacks: The Sixth Circuit Rules against Fair Use in the* MDS *Case* (1997). Available from <http://www.iupui.edu/~copyinfo/mdscase.html>.④

Crews, Kenneth D. "Federal Court's Ruling against Photocopying Chain Will Not Destroy 'Fair Use'." *Chronicle of Higher Education* 37 (April 17, 1991): A48 [analyzes the *Kinko's* case].

② *Princeton University Press v. Michigan Document Services, Inc.*, 99 F.3d 1381 (6th Cir. 1996), *cert. denied*, 520 U.S. 1156 (1997).

③ Following the final ruling in the case, the parties settled their dispute, with the copyshop paying a substantial sum of money to the publishers. More recently, Jim Smith, owner of the MDS shop, announced that he was giving up the copying business and resituating his company as a publishing firm. "Michigan Copy Shop and Publishers Settle Copyright Lawsuit," *Chronicle of Higher Education* 43 (June 20, 1997): A12; "Michigan Copy-Shop Owner Closes His Doors After Long Battle Over Copyright Law," *Chronicle of Higher Education* 44 (April 10, 1998): A14.

④ A great deal of additional information and primary-source documentation about the *MDS* case is available on the fair-use website at Stanford University Libraries: <http://fairuse.stanford.edu/mds/>.

26

Fair Use in the Courts:
More about Photocopying and Reproduction for Education

Two more cases offer insights into the meaning of fair use of potential importance to education and research needs.

Marcus v. Rowley ①

A schoolteacher prepared a twenty-four page pamphlet on cake decorating for her adult education classes. Eleven of those pages were taken directly from a copyrighted pamphlet prepared by another teacher for her classes. Even though both pamphlets were of limited circulation and were for teaching purposes only, the court held that the copying was not "fair use." Important factors in this case were that the copying was a substantial part of the original pamphlet, that the copying embraced the original pamphlet's most significant portions, and that the second pamphlet competed directly with the original pamphlet's educational purpose.

American Geophysical Union v. Texaco Inc. ②

The court ruled that photocopying of individual journal articles by a Texaco scientist for his own research needs was not fair use. In an unusual development, the court amended its opinion several months after its original issuance to limit the ruling to "systematic" copying that may advance the profit goals of the larger organization.

① *Marcus v. Rowley*, 695 F.2d 1171 (9th Cir. 1983).

② *American Geophysical Union v. Texaco Inc.*, 60 F.3d 913 (2d Cir.1994), *cert. dismissed*, 516 U.S. 1005 (1995).

Purpose: While research is generally a favored purpose, the ultimate purpose was to strengthen Texaco's corporate profits. Moreover, exact photocopies are not "transformative"; they do not build on the existing work in a productive manner.

Nature: The articles were factual, which weighs in favor of fair use.

Amount: An article is an independent work, so copying the article is copying the entire copyrighted work.

Effect: The court found no evidence that Texaco reasonably would have purchased more subscriptions to the relevant journals, but the court did conclude that non-permitted photocopying directly competes with the ability of publishers to collect license fees. According to the court, the Copyright Clearance Center (CCC) provides a practical method for paying fees and securing permissions, so the copying directly undercuts the ability to pursue the market for licensing through the CCC.

Despite an impassioned dissent from one judge who argued for the realistic needs of researchers, the court found three of the four factors weighing against fair use in the corporate context.

Sources

Consortium for Educational Technology in University Systems (CETUS). *Fair Use of Copyrighted Works: A Crucial Element in Educating America.* Seal Beach, CA: California State Univ. Chancellor's Office, 1995 [joint project of California State University, State University of New York, and City University of New York; Kenneth D. Crews, consultant and author of much of the text]. Available from <http://www.cetus.org/fairindex.html>.

Crews, Kenneth D. *Copyright Law and Graduate Research: New Media, New Rights, and Your New Dissertation.* 2d ed. Ann Arbor, MI: Bell & Howell Information and Learning, 2000. Available from <http://www.umi.com/hp/Support/DServices/copyrght/>.

For more information about the Copyright Clearance Center, visit: <http://www.copyright.com/>.

27

Fair Use and Unpublished Works

In the last several years, a series of court decisions has created a narrow application of fair use of unpublished works. The issue has been of enormous importance to the software industry and other parties, whose works are often kept "unpublished" and are worth enormous amounts of money. Yet the key cases in the courts have been about the use of letters, diaries, and other resources central to the writing of history and biography. When courts ruled that biographers may not be within fair use when making customary quotations from letters written by J.D. Salinger and L. Ron Hubbard, researchers expressed alarm.① Congress responded by adding the following sentence to the fair-use statute: "The fact that a work is unpublished shall not itself bar a finding of fair use if such finding is made upon consideration of all the above factors." The determination is back to the four factors.

The following case from 1998 demonstrates that fair use is alive and well when applied to the customary use of quotations from archival manuscripts.

Sundeman v. The Seajay Society, Inc. ②

This case is remarkable for having gone to court at all; isolated scholarly uses of materials are seldom the subject of litigation. It is also a reminder that reasonable, limited, scholarly uses of materials are most likely to be fair use. A researcher at a nonprofit

①Despite a narrow construction of fair use applied to private letters in a biographical study of J.D. Salinger, some publishers continue to brush the limits of fair use under similar circumstances. For example, when a set of letters that Salinger wrote to a former romantic acquaintance were sold at auction, news articles provided some details of their contents. Peter Applebome, "Love Letters in the Wind: A Private Affair of the Famously Private Salinger," *New York Times*, May 12, 1999, E1. When letters by Thomas Pynchon, another reclusive author, were added to the research collections of the Pierpont Morgan Library, a news article included detailed excerpts before Pynchon persuaded the library to restrict access. Mel Gussow, "Pynchon's Letters Nudge His Mask," *New York Times*, March 4, 1999, E1; Mel Gussow, "The Morgan Curtails Access to a Trove of Pynchon Letters," *New York Times*, March 21, 1998, B7.

②*Sundeman v. The Seajay Society, Inc.*, 142 F.3d 194 (4th Cir. 1998).

foundation selected quotations from an unpublished literary manuscript of historical and cultural interest, and she included those quotations in an analytical, oral presentation that she delivered to a scholarly society. The court ruled that she was acting within fair use.

Purpose: Her use was scholarly, transformative, and provided criticism and comment on the original manuscript.

Nature: The court relied on a long series of cases to resolve that the "unpublished" nature of the work "militates against" fair use.

Amount: The amount used was consistent with the purpose of scholarly criticism and commentary, and there was no evidence of taking "the heart of the work."

Effect: The court found no evidence that the presentation displaced any market for publishing the original work, and the court determined that a presentation at a scholarly conference may in fact have increased demand for the full work.

Statute and cases referenced in this chapter

Section 107 of the U.S. Copyright Act. The full text is reprinted at appendix A4.

New Era Publications Int'l., Aps. v. Henry Holt & Co., Inc., 873 F.2d 576 (2d Cir. 1989), *cert. denied*, 493 U.S. 1094 (1990) [biography of L. Ron Hubbard].

Salinger v. Random House, Inc., 811 F.2d 90 (2d Cir.), *cert. denied,* 484 U.S. 890 (1987) [biography of J.D. Salinger].

For further information

Crews, Kenneth D. "Unpublished Manuscripts and the Right of Fair Use: Copyright Law and the Strategic Management of Information Resources." *Rare Books and Manuscripts Librarianship* 5 (1990): 61-70 [written in the wake of the early decisions that tended to restrict fair use].③

Leval, Pierre N. "Toward a Fair Use Standard." *Harvard Law Review* 103 (1990): 1105-61 [Judge Leval decided the *Salinger* and the *New Era* cases while at the district court].

Wanat, Daniel E. "Fair Use and the 1992 Amendment to Section 107 of the 1976 Copyright Act: Its History and an Analysis of Its Effect." *Villanova Sports & Entertainment Law Forum* 1 (1994): 47-66.

③ For a more thorough legal analysis of these issues, see: Kenneth D. Crews, "Fair Use of Unpublished Works: Burdens of Proof and the Integrity of Copyright," *Arizona State Law Journal* 31 (1999): 3-93.

28

Experimenting with Fair Use:
Moving from Print to the Internet

A few lessons of fair use are clear: The law of fair use offers no particular boundaries or delineations. The law of fair use is also far behind the technological realities of modern education and research. We need to accept that reality. The law always lags far behind technology, and fair use is intended to be a flexible doctrine, applicable to unforeseen needs and applications.①

The preceding few chapters address copyright cases, principally for print media. We have few court rulings related to the Internet, and none tells much about fair use for educational purposes.② We are left to extrapolate from general principles and to apply our best judgment.

Electronic Reserves and Websites

Take the example of making a work available to students on the Web. It might be in the context of an "electronic-reserve" system in the library, or an individual faculty member creating websites and scanning materials for students to access for class assignments.

Copyright issues arise, particularly, when one reproduces or "scans" protected materials in order to facilitate access electronically. Other possible copyright issues include: making further copies as students print or download the material; the

①The Digital Millennium Copyright Act and the No Electronic Theft Act purport to meet the particular needs of new technologies, but for the most part they simply create new forms of rights and potential violations and raise the penalties for infringements. For closer looks at these two acts, see chapters 15 and 39.

②In a significant ruling that tells much about fair use on the Internet, a court ruled in March 2000 that an organization was not within fair use when it mounted full copies of newspaper articles on its website, even though the defendants included only select articles and offered commentary about some of them to relate the articles to the organization's not-for-profit objectives. In the end, the "nontransformative" copying of the full articles discouraged users from accessing the newspaper's website. *Los Angeles Times v. Free Republic*, 54 U.S.P.Q.2d (BNA) 1453 (C.D. Cal. 2000).

performance or display of those works when students access them at terminals; and even the possibility of making derivative works as we convert items from analog to digital format. Discussion of the copyright issues surrounding digital access could fill volumes, but here are some major issues surrounding the possible application of fair use to the loading of text and other materials onto websites or other electronic systems.

Purpose of the Use: You may strengthen the argument that your use is for nonprofit educational purposes by placing password restrictions or other limitations on access to the system. If access is limited to your students, you can more easily demonstrate educational purpose. Your systems administrator should be able to provide information and assistance with password controls at your school or campus.

Nature of the Work: We have seen that fair use generally favors nonfiction over fiction and other highly creative works. The use of scientific or other fact-based works is more likely to lean in favor of fair use than would the use of excerpts from novels, motion pictures, or other more artistic or creative materials.

Amount or Substantiality of the Use: Generally speaking, the shorter the excerpt that you use, the more likely it will be fair use. In general, be sure that you use only those amounts that are important to serving your appropriate educational purpose.

Effect on the Market: Limiting access to the system can also help reduce potential adverse effects on the market for selling copies of the original. The creative options for lessening market effects (as well as responding to the other factors) are limitless. You might limit the use to one semester; you might only use materials that are not easily available through purchase; you might select only news or academic works, rather than material from commercial monographs.

Help for Students

You might also place a helpful notice to the student users of the system, either on the screen or in materials you distribute in class. That notice might be something like this: "These materials are made available at this site for the educational purposes of students enrolled in my class at XYZ University. The materials are subject to U.S. Copyright law and are not for further reproduction or transmission."

Explain to your students in class that access to your site is limited and that they need to understand the importance of their showing respect for copyright. Abuse of copyright can lead to a loss of these opportunities for creative teaching in the future. Remember to keep in mind that fair use comes with no guarantees. There is no law to delineate what is or is not fair use for materials on "electronic reserves" or your class website. The best we can do is a reasonable application of the four factors of fair use.

The issues raised here are only a sample of the variables that may be relevant to the fair-use decision. They are a place to start when making the transition to digital applications.

For further information

Rosedale, Jeff. *Electronic Reserves Clearinghouse: Links and Materials on the Web.* Available from <http://www.cc.columbia.edu/~rosedale/>.

This site includes links to numerous colleges and universities that are implementing electronic reserve systems, and it provides links to a wealth of other sites that include helpful information about copyright issues. Some sites of special interest include those from the University of Wisconsin and the University of Texas.

The Copyright Management Center at IUPUI has developed and implemented an original policy for electronic reserves: <http://www.iupui.edu/~copyinfo/ereserves.html>.

71

29

Making Sense of Fair Use:
What About Fair-Use "Guidelines"?

The law of fair use was never intended to anticipate specific answers for individual situations. A few upcoming chapters summarize other provisions of copyright law that do provide specifics. But if the activity raises a question of fair use, the law calls on each of us to apply a set of factors to the situation. Reasonable people can and will disagree about the meaning of fair use in even the most common applications.

Educators, librarians, and others expressed concern about possible ambiguity of fair use even before Congress enacted the first fair-use statute in 1976. The result: Guidelines that attempt to define fair use as applied to common situations. Most of those guidelines are the product of negotiations among private parties holding diverse views of copyright and fair use. The first of such guidelines appeared in 1976 on the issue of photocopying for classroom handouts. In 1998 a report from the Conference on Fair Use (CONFU) proposed three more guidelines for newer technological issues.① None of these guidelines has any force of law.

Major Fair-Use Guidelines

The following is a list of the major guidelines issued by various groups since 1976, in chronological order:

①The CONFU process and the resulting guidelines proved enormously controversial and received mixed responses and levels of acceptance from interested parties. For a collection of articles examining the origins and implications of the CONFU guidelines, see: Kenneth D. Crews and Dwayne K. Buttler, eds., "Perspectives on Fair-Use Guidelines for Education and Libraries," *Journal of the American Society for Information Science* 51 (December 1999): 1303-57.

Agreement on Guidelines for Classroom Copying in Not-For-Profit Educational Institutions with Respect to Books and Periodicals, March 1976. Available from <http://www.musiclibraryassoc.org/Copyright/guidebks.htm>.

Guidelines for Educational Uses of Music, April 1976. Available from <http://www.musiclibraryassoc.org/Copyright/guidemus.htm>.

Guidelines for Off-Air Recording of Broadcast Programming for Educational Purposes, October 1981. Available from <http:// www.musiclibraryassoc.org/Copyright/guiderec.htm>.

Model Policy Concerning College and University Photocopying for Classroom, Research and Library Reserve Use, March 1982. Available from <http://www.cni.org/docs/infopols/ALA.html#mpup>.

Library and Classroom Use of Copyrighted Videotapes and Computer Software, February 1986. Available from <http://www.ifla.org/documents/infopol/copyright/ala-1.txt>.

Using Software: A Guide to the Ethical and Legal Use of Software for Members of the Academic Community, January 1992. Available from <http://www.ifla.org/documents/infopol/copyright/educom.txt>.

Fair-Use Guidelines for Electronic Reserve Systems, March 1996. Available from <http://www.cc.columbia.edu/~rosedale/guidelines.html>.

Final Report to the Commissioner on the Conclusion of the Conference on Fair Use, November 1998 [includes proposals for guidelines applicable to visual images, distance learning, and multimedia development]. Available from <http://www.uspto.gov/web/offices/dcom/olia/confu/confurep.htm>.

30

Making Sense of Fair Use:
Fair-Use Guidelines and One University's Response

The previous chapter listed several guidelines that attempt to define or explain fair use. None of those guidelines has any force of law. None of them has been enacted into law by Congress, and none has been adopted as a binding standard of fair use in any court decision. So do they present the appropriate "answer" to some fair-use problems? That question is not easily answered, and a good response could fill volumes. In the end, each individual or organization must decide for itself whether to adopt or follow any of the guidelines.

Working with Guidelines

To help with that decision, a great deal of published literature examines the merits of some of the guidelines. For example, the following book relies on the guidelines and demonstrates how they work in certain situations:

Janis H. Bruwelheide, *The Copyright Primer for Librarians and Educators* (Chicago: American Library Association, 1995).

The present writer has published works critical of many of the guidelines, arguing that they can be inappropriate for higher education and often do not accurately reflect fair use. For examples of those writings, see:

Kenneth D. Crews, *Copyright, Fair Use, and the Challenge for Universities: Promoting the Progress of Higher Education* (Chicago: University of Chicago Press, 1993).

Kenneth D. Crews, "Fair Use and Higher Education: Are Guidelines the Answer?" *Academe* 83 (November-December 1997): 38-40.

The IU Model

In response to CONFU and the earlier guidelines on fair use, Indiana University (IU) has adopted a policy based on the four factors of the law itself.[1] The IU policy on fair use, found at <http://www.iupui.edu/~copyinfo/fupolicy.html>, does not directly endorse or reject any of the guidelines, but it does caution:

> It therefore is the policy of Indiana University to facilitate the exercise in good faith of full Fair-Use rights by faculty, librarians, and staff, in furtherance of their teaching, research, and service activities. To that end, the University shall . . . avoid, whenever possible, adopting or supporting policies or agreements that would restrict Fair-Use rights. . . .[2]

The university is not prepared to instruct individuals and units that they may not follow any of the guidelines, if necessary; but the policy does urge instead a reasonable and good-faith application of the four factors of fair use: Purpose, Nature, Amount, and Effect.

A few other colleges and universities have followed the IU model, which encourages individuals to make responsible and informed application of fair use to their highly diverse and innovative teaching and

[1] A few colleges and universities have contacted the Copyright Management Center for permission to use this policy as a model for new policy at those institutions. We have been honored by the requests and pleased to give the permission. Borrowing from our policy may well be an act of fair use itself, but we are always glad to learn about an institutional decision to follow the IU example.

[2] A question has arisen occasionally about whether IU may adopt any guidelines at all on fair use in light of this policy. The answer is that the university clearly may adopt and follow guidelines. The policy prohibits restrictive standards, but the university and its units may adopt guidelines that do correspond to the actual standards of fair-use law. For example, chapter 28 mentions that IUPUI follows original, interpretative standards of fair use for electronic reserves.

research pursuits. The IU model works particularly well in an environment where decisionmaking is decentralized, and where the organization is able to provide copyright resources to facilitate responsible actions.

The Value of Factors

Basing a decision on the four factors in the statute rather than on the guidelines has profound consequences. First, the factors provide flexibility. While that flexibility might be challenging or frustrating at times, it is also important for enabling fair use to meet future needs. Second, the law of fair use includes some important protections for educators and librarians, and the only way actually to apply fair use and to secure those protections is by returning to the source of the law. That source is the statute, and it leads you to the four factors. Chapter 40 examines some of the protections for librarian and educators and emphasizes the importance of good-faith decisions.

31

Displays and Performances in Distance Learning

Brace yourself. If you never have studied copyright law for distance learning, prepare for some surprises. From the view of an educator, most of the surprises will be unwelcome. The law of distance learning has little to do with learning.

Displays and Performances

Recall from chapter 18 this statement about important exceptions to the copyright owner's rights of public display and performance of works:

> . . . the really important and good news is that the law does permit displays and performances in the context of the "face-to-face" classroom. Therefore, when we are teaching our classes in front of a group of students, we can read the text, recite the poetry, play the video, sing the songs, and even show those slides. The whole situation changes, however, when we switch from the "face-to-face" classroom and begin to transmit the materials in distance learning.

Section 110(1) of the Copyright Act provides the exception for "face-to-face" teaching; Section 110(2) applies special rules to distance learning. First, Section 110(2) lays down ground rules for the instructional program that includes displays or performances of works owned by others. Those ground rules are generally centered on the conception of distance learning as a live-time television transmission from a classroom to a few remote sites where other students are gathered. This is hardly the reality of distance learning today. When Congress enacted this law, it could not anticipate Web-based delivery and asynchronous learning experiences.

Dramatic and Nondramatic Works

Once complying with these ground rules, the law sharply delineates the works that may be transmitted. The good news is that all "displays" of works are allowed. So the instructor may show pictures, charts, graphs, text, and other still works. But "dramatic" and "nondramatic" works are treated differently, and only certain "nondramatic" works may be performed. Those terms are not defined in the law, so we have to look to common definitions.

Here are examples of works allowed to be performed under this statute:

- "Nondramatic" literary works (such as readings from textbooks, novels, and poetry); and

- "Nondramatic" musical works (such as pop music, folk music, and symphonies).①

By implication, the following works may not be performed:

- "Dramatic" literary works (such as stage plays); and

- "Dramatic" musical works (such as opera and musical theater).

Yet another complication: The law does provide a definition of "literary work," and that definition specifically excludes audiovisual works. On its face, therefore, this statute would prohibit using any

①Yet another peculiar twist of Section 110(2) is that a "musical work" is generally limited to a composition and does not include a sound recording. Technically, therefore, this statute allows performances of nondramatic compositions. Playing a recording of the work as made by a performing artist, however, may not be allowed under this code section. Oddly, that apparent gap was not a problem until recent years. When Congress enacted Section 110(2) in 1976, the "public performance" right did not apply to sound recordings at all, so an instructor could play ("perform") a recording in distance education without infringing the rights of the recording artist. As long as it was a recording of a nondramatic musical work, the use also did not infringe the composer's rights. In 1995, however, Congress created a performance right for sound recordings in the context of "digital audio transmissions." Transmitting music in distance education through digital media could now be an infringement, but the scope of Section 110(2) was not altered to reflect this new right of copyright owners. The Copyright Office Report of 1999 addresses the need to revise the statute accordingly.

audiovisual works in distance learning. Audiovisual works include feature films, educational videos, and even filmstrips.

Headaches and Reform

This statute is a headache. It draws lines that make little sense in the context of modern education. On the other hand, the language of the statute is open to some flexibility of interpretation, and you may still look to the four factors of fair use to allow activities that do not fit within Section 110(2). The papers listed below provide some elaboration.

In late 1998, Congress enacted a complex copyright bill, the Digital Millennium Copyright Act, which in part directed the U.S. Copyright Office to propose possible revisions to this statute. The Copyright Office issued its report in May 1999,[2] and it emphasized a need to revise Section 110(2) to embrace new technologies. The report is a highly thoughtful and insightful study, completed on a short deadline. It ultimately recommends to Congress that new legislation encompass the following changes:

- Expand coverage of rights to meet technological necessities.
- Allow displays and performances in the context of "mediated instruction."
- Expand the scope of allowed materials.
- Eliminate the requirement of transmitting the educational experience solely to classrooms and similar places.
- Implement safeguards to reduce risks to the copyright owners.
- Allow retention of a copy of the distance-education program on a server for access limited to students in the course during the duration of the course.
- Continue to apply fair use to activities outside the exemption for distance education.

[2] The full text of the Copyright Office Report on Distance Education is available from <http://lcweb.loc.gov/copyright/cpypub/de_rprt.pdf>.

As of this writing, Congress has yet to take any action in response to the report and proposals for change.

Source

Section 110(2) of the U.S. Copyright Act. The full text is reprinted at appendix A6.

For further information

Crews, Kenneth D. *Copyright and Distance Education: Lawful Uses of Protected Works*. Available from <http://www.ihets.org/consortium/ipse/fdhandbook/copyrt.html>.

Crews, Kenneth D. "Copyright and Distance Education: Displays, Performances, and the Limitations of Current Law." In *Growing Pains: Adapting Copyright for Libraries, Education, and Society*, ed. Laura N. Gasaway, pp. 377-94. Littleton, CO: Fred B. Rothman & Co., 1997 [an updated and revised version of the preceding article].

The Conference on Fair Use (CONFU) has proposed guidelines that attempt to apply fair use to distance learning. Those guidelines, together with comments supporting and opposing the guidelines, appear at: <http://www.uspto.gov/web/offices/dcom/olia/confu/confurep.htm>.[3]

[3] See chapter 29 for more information about CONFU and fair-use guidelines. For background about the distance-learning guidelines in particular, see: Laura N. Gasaway, "Guidelines for Distance Education and Interlibrary Loan: Doomed and More Doomed," *Journal of the American Society for Information Science* 50 (1999): 1337-41.

32

Library Copying:
A Statutory Provision of Its Own

The previous chapter examines Section 110 of the Copyright Act, which allows certain rights to use copyrighted works, in addition to the general provisions of fair use. U.S. Copyright law includes numerous such specific rights of use. Section 108 is one of those limits on the rights of the copyright owner, and it allows libraries to make and distribute copies of materials for specified purposes under specified conditions. Although meticulous, it can offer important support for library services.

Section 108 allows libraries, within limits, to make copies for purposes such as preservation, for the private study by users, and for sending in the name of "interlibrary loan." Before a library can have the benefits of Section 108, it must comply with certain general requirements and limits. Most academic and public libraries will have little trouble meeting these requirements. Other types of libraries may meet them as well.

What Are the "Ground Rules" for Section 108?

The statute establishes the following "ground rules" for making copies under Section 108:

- The library must be open to the public or to outside researchers;
- The copying must be made "without any

purpose of direct or indirect commercial advantage";

- Each copy made must include a notice of copyright; and
- The library may make only single copies on "isolated and unrelated" occasions and may not under most circumstances make multiple copies or engage in "systematic reproduction or distribution of single or multiple copies." In the case of copying for preservation purposes, the library may make up to three copies of a work.

What "Notice" Must Be on Copies?

Since passage of Section 108 in 1976, libraries and publishers have debated whether the "notice" on the copy must be the formal copyright notice found on the original (such as the notice near the beginning of this book) or some general indication of copyright's application (such as "use of this material is governed by copyright law").①

The Digital Millennium Copyright Act, enacted in late 1998, resolved this dilemma. All copies made under Section 108 must now include the notice as it appears on the original.② If no notice appears on the original then the copy only must include "a legend stating that the work may be protected by copyright."③

Are All Works Treated Equally?

The statute also sets some limits on the types of materials that libraries may copy.

If the library is making the copies for a patron's private study or for sending in interlibrary loan, the materials copied may not be:

- Musical works;
- Pictorial, graphic, sculptural works; or
- Motion pictures or audiovisual works.

① For details about the form and content of notices, see appendix D.

② A private attorney for the Association of Research Libraries has written an opinion that a library need not include on a copy of a journal article the copyright notice from the front of the journal issue. While the legal reasoning that leads to that conclusion may well prove valid, it may not provide much comfort or practical guidance to library professionals. Reprinting the notice onto the copy, or copying the notice page along with the article, requires little extra effort and much more clearly satisfies the law. For the ARL document, see < http://www.arl.org/info/frn/copy/notice.html >.

③ Suggested language for these notices is included at appendix D.

But the materials may be:

- Other types of works that are not specifically excluded (see list above);[4]
- Audiovisual works "dealing with news;" and
- Pictures and graphics "published as illustrations, diagrams, or similar adjuncts" to works that may otherwise be copied. (In other words, if you can copy the article, you can also copy the picture or chart that is in the article.)

By contrast, if the copies are for preservation of library materials, the scope of materials is not limited. Thus, for example, while audiovisual works may not be reproduced for a patron's study, they may be reproduced for preservation.

The next chapter outlines the various conditions and requirements that the library must satisfy before making copies of any materials for private study or for preservation.

Source

Section 108 of the U.S. Copyright Act. The full text of Section 108 is reprinted at appendix A5.

For further information

Gasaway, Laura N. and Sarah K. Wiant. *Libraries and Copyright: A Guide to Copyright Law in the 1990s.* Washington, D.C.: Special Libraries Association, 1994.

[4] While librarians might typically apply these provisions of Section 108 most often to textual materials, such as journal articles or books, the statute also allows the library to make copies of sound recordings. Yet often a sound recording includes a "musical work" that is separately protected by copyright law, and musical works are on the list of excluded materials. Therefore, the library can apply this part of the statute to sound recordings of works other than music, such as recordings of speeches or books on tape, and to recordings of musical works, if that musical work is now in the public domain. As always, determining whether a work is truly in the public domain can be a monstrously difficult task.

33

Library Copying:
Copies to Keep and Copies to Preserve

The previous chapter introduces Section 108 of the Copyright Act, a specific provision applicable to the making of some copies in the context of library operations.

The following are some common situations that raise questions about the meaning of Section 108:

Situation 1: Your library owns a published videotape that is now "out-of-print." The tape is well used, the images are getting weak, and the tape itself may soon break. A nearby library has a nice, clean copy. Are you allowed to copy the clean video and use it to replace your worn version?

Situation 2: The library owns technical journals on various topics, but most of them do not circulate outside the building. Library users often want photocopies of some articles for study. Whether the users may make their own copies on unsupervised machines in the library is a matter of fair use (see chapters 20 through 30). But if the library offers the service of making copies, then the activity becomes primarily a question of "library copying" under Section 108.

First, recall from chapter 32 that the library's right to make copies under Section 108 depends on complying with some not-too-onerous requirements. Second, once the library has complied with those requirements, Section 108 allows copies of certain types of materials within additional parameters.

Preservation Copying

When may the library make copies for preservation? This is the situation involving the deteriorating videotape.

If the work is unpublished, preservation copies are permitted, if:

- The copies are solely for preservation or security or for deposit at another library; and

- The work is currently in the collection of the library making the copy.①

① See Section 108(b) of the Copyright Act, reprinted at appendix A5.

If the work is previously published, preservation copies are permitted, if:

- The copies are solely for replacement of works that are damaged, deteriorating, lost, or stolen, or if the format of a work has become obsolete (e.g., a player for your collection of eight-track tapes is no longer manufactured or available for purchase); and

- The library conducts reasonable investigation to conclude that an unused replacement cannot be obtained at a fair price.②

② See Section 108(c) of the Copyright Act, reprinted at appendix A5.

Preservation in Digital Formats

Since enactment of Section 108 in 1976, librarians have pondered whether the right to make preservation copies in "facsimile form" includes the right to make digital images of deteriorating works. The Digital Millennium Copyright Act, enacted in late 1998, clarified this issue. Digital preservation copies may be made of both published and unpublished works under all the conditions set forth above. In addition, "any such copy or phonorecord that is reproduced in digital format" may not be "made available to the public in that format outside the premises of the library or archives." To oversimplify, machine-readable digital formats must be confined to the building.③

As you may recall from the previous chapter, while rights to make copies under Section 108 are often limited to textual works, the right to make preservation copies extends to other media. So you can make preservation copies of musical works, art, software, videotapes, and other works, as long as you comply with all of the requirements set forth above.

Copies for Private Study

When may the library make copies for the library user to keep? This is the situation involving the journal articles.

If the copy is an article or other portion of a larger work:

- The copy becomes the property of the user;

- The library has no notice that the copy is for any purpose other than private study, scholarship, or research; and

- The library displays a warning notice④ where orders for copies are accepted and on order forms.⑤

If the copy is of an entire work or a substantial part of it:

- The library conducts reasonable investigation to conclude that a copy cannot be obtained at a fair price;

- The copy becomes the property of the user;

③This statement is an over-simplification. For example, Section 108(b) specifies that digital technology may be used, as long as the digital copy of the work is not "otherwise" distributed or made available to the public in a digital format. Consequently, digital technology apparently may be used to make the preservation copy and to transfer it to a qualified library. Once in the library collection, the digital version then must be limited to the building.

④Appendix D offers a summary of the various notice requirements under Section 108, and it includes language that may be used for all written notices mentioned in this chapter .

⑤See Section 108(d) of the Copyright Act, reprinted at appendix A5.

- The library has no notice that the copy is for any purpose other than private study, scholarship, or research; and

- The library displays a warning notice where orders for copies are accepted and on order forms.⑥

⑥ See Section 108(e) of the Copyright Act, reprinted at appendix A5.

Copies for Interlibrary Loan

When may the library make copies to send elsewhere in the name of "interlibrary loans"?

First, a library making a copy to send to another library in the name of ILL is obliged to adhere to the general requirements above regarding the making of copies for a user's private study.⑦

⑦ See Section 108(d) and (e) of the Copyright Act, reprinted at appendix A5.

Second, the library receiving the copies must adhere to this standard: the interlibrary arrangements cannot have, as their purpose or effect, that the library receiving the copies on behalf of requesting patrons "does so in such aggregate quantities as to substitute for a subscription to or purchase of such work."⑧

⑧ See Section 108(g) of the Copyright Act, reprinted at appendix A5.

Third, to help clarify that limit on the ability to receive copies, the National Commission on New Technological Uses of Copyrighted Works (CONTU) in 1979 issued guidelines that generally allow a library to receive up to five copies of articles from the most recent five years of a journal title during one calendar year. After that quota, the general expectation is that the receiving library will pay a copyright fee or purchase its own subscription to the journal.⑨

⑨ The Conference on Fair Use (CONFU) attempted to develop guidelines to elaborate on the lawful use of digital technology for interlibrary loans. All efforts to draft guidelines failed. For background on the struggle over this issue in CONFU, see: Laura N. Gasaway, "Guidelines for Distance Education and Interlibrary Loan: Doomed and More Doomed," *Journal of the American Society for Information Science* 50 (1999): 1337-41.

For further information

Oakley, Robert, L. *Copyright and Preservation: A Serious Problem in Need of a Thoughtful Solution.* Washington, D.C.: The Commission on Preservation and Access, September 1990. Available from <http://www.ilt.columbia.edu/text_version/projects/copyright/papers/oakley.html>.

U.S. Copyright Office. *Reproduction of Copyrighted Works by Educators and Librarians, Circular 21.* Washington D.C.: U.S. Copyright Office, September 1995 [includes full text of the CONTU guidelines]. Available from <http://lcweb.loc.gov/copyright/circs/circ21.pdf>.

34

Library Copying:
Copy Machines in the Library

A Common Scenario: The library provides unsupervised photocopy machines, where users make their own copies. The librarians will not even know what they are copying. Is the library liable for infringements committed on machines that the library provides?

Simple answer: No, but only if . . . .

Section 108(f)(1) of the Copyright Act specifically addresses this issue. As long as the library displays a notice informing users that making copies may be subject to copyright law, the statute releases the library and its staff from liability in most situations, but the user of the machine is still responsible for any infringements. That person could be you.

So what may you copy on that machine and still avoid liability? The answer in most instances lies in the four factors of fair use, detailed in earlier messages. (Even though you may be making the copies at a location inside the library, Section 108 generally applies only to copying made *by* the library, not necessarily all copying *at* the library.)

Also note that the statute offers this protection only to libraries that post notices on unsupervised "reproducing equipment" at the library. The statute does not refer only to photocopy machines. A library ought to post the notice on all unsupervised photocopy machines, as well as on VCRs, tape decks, microfilm readers, computers, printers, and any other equipment that is capable of making copies.

What should the notice state? The law does not prescribe the text of any notice. Use your good judgment. Most often you might see general statements about copyright. No more is likely required.①

Source

Section 108 of the U.S. Copyright Act. The full text of Section 108 is reprinted at Appendix A5.

For further information

University of Texas, Copyright Crash Course. "Copyright in the Library." Available from <http://www.utsystem.edu/ogc/intellectualproperty/l-intro.htm>.

① A form of notice commonly used in libraries states: "Notice: The copyright law of the United States (Title 17, U.S. Code) governs the making of photocopies or other reproductions of copyrighted material. The person using this equipment is liable for any infringement."

35

Copyright and New Technologies: Computer Software

Copyright law does apply to computer software, whether in the form of source code or as digitally embodied on disk. When Congress explicitly extended the law to encompass software, it also recognized that software use requires some special deference. As a result, Section 117 of the U.S. Copyright Act generally assures that the owner of a copy of computer software may make a backup copy of it to protect the software from loss or damage. That section also allows the owner of the copy to make modifications that are an "essential step" to using the software on specific hardware equipment. Thus, if you purchased a software package, you may alter or otherwise adapt the particular copy in order to make it work on your computer's platform or operating system, or to meet other particular requirements of your computer.[1]

The right to make backup copies, however, is limited to "software," which is generally defined to mean programming that governs the operation of the computer. This right does not necessarily apply to disks or coding that include text, images, and other works.

> [1] The Digital Millennium Copyright Act (DMCA), enacted in October 1998, revised Section 117 to provide that an owner of a software program may also make a copy of it in connection with repairing the computer on which the software is loaded. This statutory change is a direct response to *MAI Sys. Corp. v. Peak Computer, Inc.*, 991 F.2d 511 (9th Cir. 1993), which held that such a copy was an infringement.

Fair Use of Software

The concept of fair use for software is not easy. One of the problems you are likely to encounter is that conventional articulations of fair-use analysis often make little sense when applied to reproductions of the full software program or when the reproduction of the software program is a clear substitution for purchasing a software package. Indeed, software producers and universities sometimes have been enormously successful in working around these issues by providing site licenses for software programs at reasonable rates. Often these licenses permit installing many programs on hundreds or thousands of machines around our campuses and at home.

On the other hand, fair use may allow experimental uses of software, especially under tightly controlled conditions. For example, fair use may allow students or researchers to decompile the programming to learn how it works.② Fair use may allow brief clips from programs or screen displays for scholarly studies. Apply the four factors of fair use to your situation.

Growth of Licensing

Licenses and other agreements also increasingly determine software use.③ The enforceability of "shrink-wrap" or "click-on" licenses in common situations is still open to debate. It is possible, however, by agreement made at the time of acquiring the program, to have consented to standards of behavior that may either expand your rights under the law or take them away. Be sure to read what you sign, and do not hesitate to negotiate.④

Source

Section 117 of the U.S. Copyright Act. The full text is available from the Copyright Management website: <http://www.iupui.edu/~copyinfo/sec117.html>.

For further information

Software & Information Industry Association. *Copyright Law & Related Issues* [industry view of software issues]. Available from <http://www.siia.net/piracy/copyright/>.

②Decompiling computer software has become even more problematic after passage of the DMCA. One of the act's provisions prohibits the "circumvention" of "technological protection systems." Thus, if software includes restrictions blocking access to the underlying code, circumventing those restrictions can be a violation of the law, even if the ultimate use of the work is still fair use. See chapter 15.

③Licenses are likely to become more common and more readily enforceable if states adopt the Uniform Computer Information Transactions Act (UCITA), which generally would enforce licenses, including shrink-wrap licenses, even if they restrict fair use and other rights established under federal copyright law.

④Whether or not you read all the fine print, and regardless of its enforceability, terms and restrictions and other identifying information can be "copyright management information," and under the DMCA removal of that information under some circumstances can be a federal violation. See chapter 15.

36

Copyright and New Technologies: The World Wide Web

The World Wide Web and Internet sites are hardly immune from copyright. One of the common myths about copyright is that the public's unrestricted access to the Web places the content of a website into the public domain. That conclusion is absolutely false and a complete misunderstanding of current copyright law.

Protection for Your Website

Remember that copyright protection vests automatically to original works that are fixed in a tangible medium (see chapters 3 to 5). Thus, when you create original text, images, and other materials for a website, you are most likely creating original works that are fixed in some tangible medium. A tangible medium may be print or electronic. It may be a Web server or a floppy disk.

Therefore, copyright protects almost everything you may find on the Web. The decision to place material on the Web and to give unrestricted access does not put it in the public domain. The lack of any copyright notice on the work also does not put it in the public domain under today's law.

As you build your own website, you need to consider the issues related to copyright protection of your work, including appropriate notice on the homepage and even the possibility of registering the work with the U.S. Copyright Office.① More about those issues appears in chapters 8 and 9.

① On the website for the U.S. Copyright Office, you can find information and forms for registering a website. Look in particular at Circular 66, "Copyright Registration for Online works," available from <http://lcweb.loc.gov/copyright/circs/circ66.pdf>.

Fair Use on the Web

On the other hand, copyright-protected material on the Web is also subject to fair use and other "limitations" on the rights of the copyright owner. The circumstances of unrestricted Web access may influence analysis of the four factors of fair use (see chapters 19 to 23). Unconditional public access to materials voluntarily placed on the Web by the copyright owner may easily tip some of the four factors in favor of fair use in some situations.②

For example, in evaluating the nature of the work, unlimited availability on the Web is one attribute of the work, and it is an attribute that implies that the copyright owner accepts and understands that the public will have relatively easy and liberal access to the work and the ability to use it. In addition, the unrestricted availability of the work on the Web without an indication of claiming a market for the work implies that the copyright owner is not seeking to secure any potential revenue from the work directly.③

By contrast, broad and easy access via the Web may also limit the scope of fair use as you include someone else's copyrighted pictures or clips of words or sound in your Web project. Worldwide access to the project may draw into question the legitimate purpose of the use and its effect on the market for or value of the original work. For more information about fair use and placing materials on the Web, see chapter 28.

Always keep in mind when applying fair use that you must weigh in the balance all of the relevant facts and all four of the factors. Do not rush to a conclusion based on, for example, just two of the factors and the few facts reviewed here.

For further information

University of Virginia Library, Digital Media Center [includes links to copyright resources about digital media]. Available from <http://www.lib.virginia.edu/dmc/>.

② Ordinarily, simple linking to a site is not likely grounds for an infringement claim, because linking usually is not equivalent to reproducing the work or exercising any other rights of the copyright owner. A recent case held that a website operator is liable for "contributory infringement" when, after the court ordered the operator to remove infringing materials from its site, the operator then posted information explaining where to find the same materials on other sites and encouraged users to locate and further disseminate the copyrighted works. *Intellectual Reserve v. Utah Lighthouse Ministry, Inc.*, 75 F. Supp.2d 1290 (D. Utah 1999).

③ On the other hand, the case involving the *Los Angeles Times* (see chapter 28), suggests that the market is not necessarily the sale of a particular article found on the website, but rather the general traffic that articles can draw to the newspaper's site. Similarly, in *Kelly v. Arriba Soft Corp.*, 77 F. Supp.2d 1116, 1120 (C.D. Cal. 1999), the court ruled in a case involving the use of photographs found on the Web: "The relevant market is the plaintiff's web site as a whole. . . . The value of the plaintiff's photographs to plaintiff could potentially be adversely affected if their promotional purposes are undermined."

37

Requesting Permission
from the Copyright Owner

Now you have made the full copyright analysis. If your use is either unrestricted or "fair," you may proceed without further ado. If your proposed use exceeds fair use, you need permission from the copyright owner. Prepare a direct and concise letter; you will find a sample form at a website listed below.

A Good Letter

A good permission letter includes a thorough description of the material to be used and a detailed explanation of how it will be used. The letter also includes a place for the recipient to sign indicating that permission is granted. You need to have an affirmative response. Silence is not permission.

Perhaps the most important part of the letter is the addressee. You may need to spend considerable effort identifying the actual copyright owner. The creator of a new work owns the copyright at its inception, but copyrights may be sold, given away, or assigned. Writers frequently transfer copyright privileges to their publishers. Most published works do include a copyright notice, which should indicate the original claimant of ownership. Contact the party named in the notice.

Throughout this process, the telephone can be your most efficient ally. Before sending any letter, call to confirm the address and the name of someone to address personally. Call to be sure you have found the current copyright owner. Call to be sure the recipient understands the copyright issues and will cooperate in granting permission. Copyright owners may request a fee for the permission—ranging from nominal to prohibitive. You need to decide whether your use of the material is sufficiently important to justify the fee. Common courtesy means thanking the grantors in an acknowledgment section of your work.

Licensing Agents

Other possibilities are available for securing permission to use some works in some situations. For example, the Copyright Clearance Center provides a fairly expedient means for securing permission to use materials, often for educational purposes. The CCC acts as a licensing agent on behalf of numerous publishers and other copyright owners to grant permissions, usually for photocopying, but increasingly for electronic duplication. BMI, ASCAP, and various other organizations license certain uses of musical works on behalf of composers and recording artists. You can expect that these organizations will charge a fee for their services. You should always feel free to contact the copyright owner directly. You may get the permission you need without cost. It never hurts to try.

Source

Crews, Kenneth D. *Copyright Law and Graduate Research: New Media, New Rights, and Your New Dissertation.* 2d ed. Ann Arbor, MI: Bell & Howell Information and Learning, 2000 [includes a sample permission letter]. Available from <http://www.umi.com/hp/Support/DServices/copyrght/>.

For further information

For information about the Copyright Clearance Center, visit <http://www.copyright.com>.

38

Liability for Copyright Infringement

Thus far, this entire book has carefully avoided the topic of liability for copyright infringement. The absence of liability issues is no accident. This book's fundamental objective is to educate readers in order to prepare them to handle copyright situations in an informed and good-faith manner, thereby avoiding liability.

Yet the time may come when you might have infringed the rights of the copyright owner (e.g., you "reproduced" a protected work without permission and in a manner that is not within fair use or another exception). You may be held legally responsible. Perhaps instead you are the copyright owner, asserting a claim against a purported infringer.[1]

Who Is Liable for Infringements?

In the first place, the person who actually commits the infringement is liable. That person might be the librarian filling orders for copies, a research assistant duplicating materials for a professor, or the webmaster creating a "cut-and-paste" website. In general, liability begins with the person who pushes the button to make the copies. In reality, liability often flows upstream to the supervisors who oversee the project and to the company or organization itself. Recall some of the summaries of cases about fair use. The liable parties were the corporations—such as Kinko's and Texaco—and not necessarily the individuals (see chapters 24 to 26).

[1] This message offers a brief summary of the provisions of the DMCA that relate to the liability of Online Service Providers. Those provisions are vastly more complex than can be summarized here. More information about the DMCA and the OSP provisions is contained in appendices B and F.

Liability of Service Providers

Is America Online or even your university or library responsible for any infringement committed by faculty, students, or others who make unlawful uses of materials in their email or on their websites?

Case law on this issue is slowly evolving.② A large, public-access provider such as AOL may well be merely a communication network and not be responsible for many infringements committed by customers. A company or university may face a bit more difficult challenge when infringements are committed by employees. Often an employer shares the liability for the misdeeds of employees.

The Digital Millennium Copyright Act (DMCA) addressed the question of online service provider (OSP) liability.③ The law does not resolve the issue, but instead offers a "safe harbor" for universities and other OSPs. To enjoy that protection, the OSP must meet a lengthy list of elaborate conditions.④ Moreover, the "safe harbor" only protects the university from liability for copyright infringements committed by faculty and some other users of the system. The individuals are still liable. Other legal claims—trademark, privacy, libel—may also still pass through to the institution.

For educational institutions, fitting into the safe harbor at all may prove highly problematic. In addition to the foregoing conditions, the "safe harbor" might apply to a faculty website only if the infringing materials on the site were not "required or recommended" course materials within the last three years, and the institution has received no more than two notifications of claimed infringements committed by that faculty member. The institution also must provide all users of its system materials that "accurately describe, and promote compliance with" copyright law.

This summary is only a sample of the law's complexity. Future experience will tell much about

② For examples of recent cases brought against service providers, see:

Playboy v. Hardenburgh, 982 F. Supp. 503 (N.D. Ohio 1997) (online "bulletin board" operator that screened posted materials found liable for direct and contributory copyright infringement on basis of knowledge of infringing materials).

Religious Technology Center v. NETCOM, 907 F. Supp. 1361 (N.D. Cal. 1995) (OSP not liable for direct infringement resulting from automatic copying and caching performed by equipment).

For one view of the need for an OSP exemption, see: Daniel Cahoy, "New Legislation Regarding On-Line Service Provider Liability for Copyright Infringement: A Solution in Search of a Problem," *IDEA* 38 (1998): 335-60.

③ The provisions related to the liability of OSPs are codified at Section 512 of the U.S. Copyright Act.

④ For any OSP, the technical and technological conditions are numerous. For example, the OSP must be unaware of the possible infringement, and the computer network must be implemented in a manner that accommodates identifying marks or tags on the transmitted materials. The OSP must also have and implement a policy that terminates network privileges for "repeat infringers," although the law does not define who they might be. The list of conditions reaches far beyond these examples. For further details see appendix B.

its feasibility, whether it will achieve the intended purposes, and whether courts will use it to create meaningful protection for service providers that seek to facilitate information flow.

For further information ⑤

Crews, Kenneth D. *President Signs New Criminal Copyright Bill: Raising the Stakes for Electronic Copyright Responsibilities* (1997) [summarizes and analyzes the 1997 amendment to the Copyright Act]. Available from <http://www.iupui.edu/~copyinfo/noetheft.html>.

⑤ The source listed below summarizes recent legislation that imposed stiffer criminal penalties for copyright infringement. In yet a more recent bill, Congress directed the U.S. Sentencing Commission to establish sentencing guidelines for criminal infringements. In the hearings leading to that legislation, some members of Congress were concerned that only a few prosecutions against infringers had occurred since passage of the 1997 bill.

39

What Is at Stake
in an Infringement Action?

What is at stake in an infringement action? In the unlikely event of a court ruling that you have committed an infringement, the consequences can be staggering. An injunction can bar further infringements, the court can impound the copies and your equipment, and you can be ordered to reimburse the losses that the copyright owner incurred or pay the profits you gained from the wrongdoing.

Damages and Registration

The copyright owner who successfully makes an infringement claim is also entitled to receive two more "remedies" that involve significant dollars. First, the owner can seek "statutory damages" of up to $30,000 per work infringed, in lieu of actual damages.[1] Second, the owner can also ask for reimbursement of attorney fees.

Now pause here for a second. Recall this statement from chapter 8 about registering a work with the U.S. Copyright Office:

> Do not overlook the benefits of formalities for your new works. Placing the copyright notice on your work offers valuable information to the reader. Registering a claim with the U.S. Copyright Office gives you important legal benefits in the unlikely event of a lawsuit.

[1] The Digital Theft Deterrence and Copyright Damages Improvement Act of 1999, Public Law No. 106-160, 113 Stat. 1774, increased the potential statutory damage amounts from $20,000 to $30,000, and in the event of "willful infringement," Congress increased the amount from $100,000 to $150,000.

The financial benefits of statutory damages and attorney fees are generally available to the copyright owner only if the owner registered the work before the infringement occurred. Hence, a clear lesson to copyright owners: You may well be the copyright owner without attending to the formalities of registration, but without registration you are not entitled to what may be the most lucrative remedies for infringement.

If the infringement is "willful," the consequences skyrocket. Criminal liability may also apply. Moreover, Congress amended the Copyright Act in late 1997 to add tougher criminal liabilities for "willful" infringements, especially in electronic media.[2]

Sovereign Immunity

Liability, dollars, and jail are disturbing. The next chapter offers some crucial pointers for how to advance productive activities, while at the same time not living in unfounded fear of liability. Here is one other recent development that reshapes the issue for many educators and librarians.

The Eleventh Amendment to the U.S. Constitution provides that a state or state agency may not be sued in federal courts for dollar damages.[3] A series of recent cases from the U.S. Supreme Court has brought renewed meaning to the provision, which is intended to protect the "sovereign" of the states from being held accountable by a federal judiciary. The problem is that by act of Congress all copyright cases must be brought in federal court. In recent years, courts have dismissed many cases brought against states and state agencies in federal court. Of particular note, a court ruled in February 2000 that a unit of the University of Houston (a public university) could therefore not be sued for copyright infringement.[4]

[2] This act also strives to clarify the type and severity of sentences given for "willful" criminal infringement by directing a study of this issue by the United States Sentencing Commission.

[3] The Eleventh Amendment provides: "The Judicial power of the United States shall not be construed to extend to any suit in law or equity, commenced or prosecuted against one of the United States by Citizens of another State, or by Citizens or Subjects of any Foreign State."

[4] *Chavez v. Arte Publico Press*, 204 F.3d 601 (5th Cir. 2000).

While these developments may give some luxury to states and state institutions to consider the appropriateness of their activities—rather than acting out of fear of liability—these cases by no means give public institutions complete protection. They may still be liable for equitable remedies, such as injunctions, and if a public university acted in willful disregard of the law, it could face criminal action. Moreover, educators and librarians are increasingly concerned about protecting their own intellectual property. Fairness and ethics demand a mutual respect for the interests of others.

For further information

Crews, Kenneth D. *President Signs New Criminal Copyright Bill: Raising the Stakes for Electronic Copyright Responsibilities* (1997) [summarizes and analyzes the 1997 amendment to the Copyright Act]. Available from <http://www.iupui.edu/~copyinfo/ noetheft.html>.

Crews, Kenneth D. and Georgia K. Harper. "The Immunity Dilemma: Are State Colleges and Universities Still Liable for Copyright Infringements?" *Journal of the American Society for Information Science* 50 (December 1999): 1350-52.

40

Acting in Good Faith

With a variety of potential legal liabilities hanging over our heads, how can we reasonably live amidst the uncertainty that copyright sometimes brings? The best bet: Act in an informed and good-faith manner.

That basic advice may seem trivial, but it is actually of central importance, particularly for educators and librarians working with fair use. Reasonable people can and will disagree about the meaning of fair use. Congress recognized that it was enacting a law open to significant differences of interpretation, so Congress provided an important safety valve for educators and librarians.

Reasonable Grounds

Recall from the last chapter that one of the possible remedies for infringement is "statutory damages" of up to $30,000 per work infringed.[1] Imagine you are in front of the judge, who has just ruled that you are an infringer and is preparing to assess damages. The law of statutory damages further provides that if you are an employee or agent of a nonprofit educational institution or library, acting within the scope of employment, and you "believed and had reasonable grounds for believing" that the copies you made were "fair use," the court must remit the statutory damages.[2]

[1] The Digital Theft Deterrence and Copyright Damages Improvement Act of 1999, Public Law No. 106-160, 113 Stat. 1774, increased the potential statutory damage amounts from $20,000 to $30,000, and in the event of "willful infringement," Congress increased the amount from $100,000 to $150,000.

[2] The law of statutory damages and the exception for educators and librarians are set forth in Section 504(c) of the U.S. Copyright Act, reprinted at appendix A7.

You are not completely off the hook. You are still an infringer subject to all other remedies. Further, the exception for librarians and educators does not cover all possible uses of copyrighted materials. Nevertheless, one big piece of potential liability is gone if you acted in good faith—if you believed you were within fair use, and you had "reasonable grounds" for that belief.

The Value of Learning

How do you attain the "reasonable grounds"? By learning. You do not have to become an expert. You already have learned a good amount about fair use through this book. Keep yourself informed and make reasonable decisions about fair use, and you may find that much of the potential liability is gone. You may also find that your good judgment—especially a decision based on a balancing of the four factors of fair use—means that you really are within fair use.

For further information

Oakes, James L. "Copyrights and Copyremedies: Unfair Use and Injunctions." *Hofstra Law Review* 18 (1990): 983-1003.

Appendix A

Selected Provisions from the
U.S. Copyright Act

Appendix A1
§ 101. Definitions

Except as otherwise provided in this title, as used in this title, the following terms and their variant forms mean the following:

. . .

"Audiovisual works" are works that consist of a series of related images which are intrinsically intended to be shown by the use of machines or devices such as projectors, viewers, or electronic equipment, together with accompanying sounds, if any, regardless of the nature of the material objects, such as films or tapes, in which the works are embodied.

. . .

A "collective work" is a work, such as a periodical issue, anthology, or encyclopedia, in which a number of contributions, constituting separate and independent works in themselves, are assembled into a collective whole.

A "compilation" is a work formed by the collection and assembling of preexisting materials or of data that are selected, coordinated, or arranged in such a way that the resulting work as a whole constitutes an original work of authorship. The term "compilation" includes collective works.

105

"Copies" are material objects, other than phonorecords, in which a work is fixed by any method now known or later developed, and from which the work can be perceived, reproduced, or otherwise communicated, either directly or with the aid of a machine or device. The term "copies" includes the material object, other than a phonorecord, in which the work is first fixed.
. . .

A work is "created" when it is fixed in a copy or phonorecord for the first time; where a work is prepared over a period of time, the portion of it that has been fixed at any particular time constitutes the work as of that time, and where the work has been prepared in different versions, each version constitutes a separate work.

A "derivative work" is a work based upon one or more preexisting works, such as a translation, musical arrangement, dramatization, fictionalization, motion picture version, sound recording, art reproduction, abridgment, condensation, or any other form in which a work may be recast, transformed, or adapted. A work consisting of editorial revisions, annotations, elaborations, or other modifications, which, as a whole, represent an original work of authorship, is a "derivative work".

A "device", "machine", or "process" is one now known or later developed.

A "digital transmission" is a transmission in whole or in part in a digital or other non-analog format.

To "display" a work means to show a copy of it, either directly or by means of a film, slide, television image, or any other device or process or, in the case of a motion picture or other audiovisual work, to show individual images nonsequentially.
. . .

A work is "fixed" in a tangible medium of expression when its embodiment in a copy or phonorecord, by or under the authority of the author, is sufficiently permanent or stable to permit it to be perceived, reproduced, or otherwise communicated for a period of more than transitory duration. A work consisting of sounds, images, or both, that are being transmitted, is "fixed" for purposes of this title if a fixation of the work is being made simultaneously with its transmission.
. . .

A "joint work" is a work prepared by two or more authors with the intention that their contributions be merged into inseparable or interdependent parts of a unitary whole.

"Literary works" are works, other than audiovisual works, expressed in words, numbers, or other verbal or numerical symbols or indicia, regardless of the nature of the material objects, such as books, periodicals, manuscripts, phonorecords, film, tapes, disks, or cards, in which they are embodied.

"Motion pictures" are audiovisual works consisting of a series of related images which, when shown in succession, impart an impression of motion, together with accompanying sounds, if any.

To "perform" a work means to recite, render, play, dance, or act it, either directly or by means of any device or process or, in the case of a motion picture or other audiovisual work, to show its images in any sequence or to make the sounds accompanying it audible.

. . .

"Phonorecords" are material objects in which sounds, other than those accompanying a motion picture or other audiovisual work, are fixed by any method now known or later developed, and from which the sounds can be perceived, reproduced, or otherwise communicated, either directly or with the aid of a machine or device. The term "phonorecords" includes the material object in which the sounds are first fixed.

"Pictorial, graphic, and sculptural works" include two-dimensional and three-dimensional works of fine, graphic, and applied art, photographs, prints and art reproductions, maps, globes, charts, diagrams, models, and technical drawings, including architectural plans. Such works shall include works of artistic craftsmanship insofar as their form but not their mechanical or utilitarian aspects are concerned; the design of a useful article, as defined in this section, shall be considered a pictorial, graphic, or sculptural work only if, and only to the extent that, such design incorporates pictorial, graphic, or sculptural features that can be identified separately from, and are capable of existing independently of, the utilitarian aspects of the article.

. . .

"Publication" is the distribution of copies or phonorecords of a work to the public by sale or other transfer of ownership, or by rental, lease, or lending. The offering to distribute copies or phonorecords to a group of persons for purposes of further distribution, public performance, or public display, constitutes publication. A public performance or display of a work does not of itself constitute publication.

To perform or display a work "publicly" means—
(1) to perform or display it at a place open to the public or at any place where a substantial number of persons outside of a normal circle of a family and its social acquaintances is gathered; or
(2) to transmit or otherwise communicate a performance or display of the work to a place specified by clause (1) or to the public, by means of any device or process, whether the members of the public capable of receiving the performance or display receive it in the same place or in separate places and at the same time or at different times.

. . .

"Sound recordings" are works that result from the fixation of a series of musical, spoken, or other sounds, but not including the sounds accompanying a motion picture or other audiovisual work, regardless of the nature of the material objects, such as disks, tapes, or other phonorecords, in which they are embodied.

. . .

A "transfer of copyright ownership" is an assignment, mortgage, exclusive license, or any other conveyance, alienation, or hypothecation of a copyright or of any of the exclusive rights comprised in a copyright, whether or not it is limited in time or place of effect, but not including a nonexclusive license.

To "transmit" a performance or display is to communicate it by any device or process whereby images or sounds are received beyond the place from which they are sent.

. . .

A "work of visual art" is—

(1) a painting, drawing, print or sculpture, existing in a single copy, in a limited edition of 200 copies or fewer that are signed and consecutively numbered by the author, or, in the case of a sculpture, in multiple cast, carved, or fabricated sculptures of 200 or fewer that are consecutively numbered by the author and bear the signature or other identifying mark of the author; or

(2) a still photographic image produced for exhibition purposes only, existing in a single copy that is signed by the author, or in a limited edition of 200 copies or fewer that are signed and consecutively numbered by the author.

A work of visual art does not include—

(A)(i) any poster, map, globe, chart, technical drawing, diagram, model, applied art, motion picture or other audiovisual work, book, magazine, newspaper, periodical, data base, electronic information service, electronic publication, or similar publication;

(ii) any merchandising item or advertising, promotional, descriptive, covering, or packaging material or container;

(iii) any portion or part of any item described in clause (i) or (ii);

(B) any work made for hire; or

(C) any work not subject to copyright protection under this title.

A "work of the United States Government" is a work prepared by an officer or employee of the United States Government as part of that person's official duties.

A "work made for hire" is—

(1) a work prepared by an employee within the scope of his or her employment; or

(2) a work specially ordered or commissioned for use as a contribution to a collective work, as a part of a motion picture or other audiovisual work as a sound recording, as a translation, as a supplementary work, as a compilation, as an instructional text, as a test, as answer material for a test, or as an atlas, if the parties expressly agree in a written instrument signed by them that the work shall be considered a work made for hire. For the purpose of the foregoing sentence, a "supplementary work" is a work prepared for publication as a secondary adjunct to a work by another author for the purpose of introducing, concluding, illustrating, explaining, revising, commenting upon, or assisting in the use of the other work, such as forewords, afterwords, pictorial illustrations, maps, charts, tables, editorial notes, musical arrangements, answer material for tests, bibliographies, appendixes, and indexes, and an "instructional text" is a literary,

pictorial, or graphic work prepared for publication and with the purpose of use in systematic instructional activities. The terms "WTO Agreement" and "WTO member country" have the meanings given those terms in paragraphs (9) and (10), respectively, of section 2 of the Uruguay Round Agreements Act.

. . .

A "computer program" is a set of statements or instructions to be used directly or indirectly in a computer in order to bring about a certain result.

Appendix A2
§ 102. Subject Matter of Copyright: In General

(a) Copyright protection subsists, in accordance with this title, in original works of authorship fixed in any tangible medium of expression, now known or later developed, from which they can be perceived, reproduced, or otherwise communicated, either directly or with the aid of a machine or device. Works of authorship include the following categories:

 (1) literary works;
 (2) musical works, including any accompanying words;
 (3) dramatic works, including any accompanying music;
 (4) pantomimes and choreographic works;
 (5) pictorial, graphic, and sculptural works;
 (6) motion pictures and other audiovisual works;
 (7) sound recordings; and
 (8) architectural works.

(b) In no case does copyright protection for an original work of authorship extend to any idea, procedure, process, system, method of operation, concept, principle, or discovery, regardless of the form in which it is described, explained, illustrated, or embodied in such work.

Appendix A3
§ 106. Exclusive Rights in Copyrighted Works

Subject to sections 107 through 120, the owner of copyright under this title has the exclusive rights to do and to authorize any of the following:

 (1) to reproduce the copyrighted work in copies or phonorecords;
 (2) to prepare derivative works based upon the copyrighted work;
 (3) to distribute copies or phonorecords of the copyrighted work to the public by sale or other transfer of ownership, or by rental, lease, or lending;
 (4) in the case of literary, musical, dramatic, and choreographic works, pantomimes, and motion pictures and other audiovisual works, to perform the

copyrighted work publicly;

(5) in the case of literary, musical, dramatic, and choreographic works, pantomimes, and pictorial, graphic, or sculptural works, including the individual images of a motion picture or other audiovisual work, to display the copyrighted work publicly; and

(6) in the case of sound recordings, to perform the copyrighted work publicly by means of a digital audio transmission.

Appendix A4
§ 107. Limitations on Exclusive Rights: Fair Use

Notwithstanding the provisions of sections 106 and 106A, the fair use of a copyrighted work, including such use by reproduction in copies or phonorecords or by any other means specified by that section, for purposes such as criticism, comment, news reporting, teaching (including multiple copies for classroom use), scholarship, or research, is not an infringement of copyright. In determining whether the use made of a work in any particular case is a fair use the factors to be considered shall include —

(1) the purpose and character of the use, including whether such use is of a commercial nature or is for nonprofit educational purposes;

(2) the nature of the copyrighted work;

(3) the amount and substantiality of the portion used in relation to the copyrighted work as a whole; and

(4) the effect of the use upon the potential market for or value of the copyrighted work.

The fact that a work is unpublished shall not itself bar a finding of fair use if such finding is made upon consideration of all the above factors.

Appendix A5
§ 108. Limitations on Exclusive Rights:
Reproduction by Libraries and Archives

(a) Except as otherwise provided in this title and notwithstanding the provisions of section 106, it is not an infringement of copyright for a library or archives, or any of its employees acting within the scope of their employment, to reproduce no more than one copy or phonorecord of a work, except as provided in subsections (b) and (c), or to distribute such copy or phonorecord, under the conditions specified by this section, if—

(1) the reproduction or distribution is made without any purpose of direct or indirect commercial advantage;

(2) the collections of the library or archives are (i) open to the public, or (ii) available not only to researchers affiliated with the library or archives or with the institution of which it is a part, but also to other persons doing research in a specialized

field; and

(3) the reproduction or distribution of the work includes a notice of copyright that appears on the copy or phonorecord that is reproduced under the provisions of this section, or includes a legend stating that the work may be protected by copyright if no such notice can be found on the copy or phonorecord that is reproduced under the provisions of this section.

(b) The rights of reproduction and distribution under this section apply to three copies or phonorecords of an unpublished work duplicated solely for purposes of preservation and security or for deposit for research use in another library or archives of the type described by clause (2) of subsection (a), if—

(1) the copy or phonorecord reproduced is currently in the collections of the library or archives; and

(2) any such copy or phonorecord that is reproduced in digital format is not otherwise distributed in that format and is not made available to the public in that format outside the premises of the library or archives.

(c) The right of reproduction under this section applies to three copies or phonorecords of a published work duplicated solely for the purpose of replacement of a copy or phonorecord that is damaged, deteriorating, lost, or stolen, or if the existing format in which the work is stored has become obsolete, if—

(1) the library or archives has, after a reasonable effort, determined that an unused replacement cannot be obtained at a fair price; and

(2) any such copy or phonorecord that is reproduced in digital format is not made available to the public in that format outside the premises of the library or archives in lawful possession of such copy.

For purposes of this subsection, a format shall be considered obsolete if the machine or device necessary to render perceptible a work stored in that format is no longer manufactured or is no longer reasonably available in the commercial marketplace.

(d) The rights of reproduction and distribution under this section apply to a copy, made from the collection of a library or archives where the user makes his or her request or from that of another library or archives, of no more than one article or other contribution to a copyrighted collection or periodical issue, or to a copy or phonorecord of a small part of any other copyrighted work, if—

(1) the copy or phonorecord becomes the property of the user, and the library or archives has had no notice that the copy or phonorecord would be used for any purpose other than private study, scholarship, or research; and

(2) the library or archives displays prominently, at the place where orders are accepted, and includes on its order form, a warning of copyright in accordance with requirements that the Register of Copyrights shall prescribe by regulation.

(e) The rights of reproduction and distribution under this section apply to the entire work, or to a substantial part of it, made from the collection of a library or archives where the user makes his or her request or from that of another library or archives, if the library or archives has first determined, on the basis of a reasonable investigation, that a copy or phonorecord of the copyrighted work cannot be obtained at a fair price, if—

(1) the copy or phonorecord becomes the property of the user, and the library or archives has had no notice that the copy or phonorecord would be used for any purpose other than private study, scholarship, or research; and

(2) the library or archives displays prominently, at the place where orders are accepted, and includes on its order form, a warning of copyright in accordance with requirements that the Register of Copyrights shall prescribe by regulation.

(f) Nothing in this section—

(1) shall be construed to impose liability for copyright infringement upon a library or archives or its employees for the unsupervised use of reproducing equipment located on its premises: *Provided,* That such equipment displays a notice that the making of a copy may be subject to the copyright law;

(2) excuses a person who uses such reproducing equipment or who requests a copy or phonorecord under subsection (d) from liability for copyright infringement for any such act, or for any later use of such copy or phonorecord; if it exceeds fair use as provided by section 107;

(3) shall be construed to limit the reproduction and distribution by lending of a limited number of copies and excerpts by a library or archives of an audiovisual news program, subject to clauses (1), (2), and (3) of subsection (a); or

(4) in any way affects the right of fair use as provided by section 107, or any contractual obligations assumed at any time by the library or archives when it obtained a copy or phonorecord of a work in its collections.

(g) The rights of reproduction and distribution under this section extend to the isolated and unrelated reproduction or distribution of a single copy or phonorecord of the same material on separate occasions, but do not extend to cases where the library or archives, or its employee—

(1) is aware or has substantial reason to believe that it is engaging in the related or concerted reproduction or distribution of multiple copies or phonorecords of the same material, whether made on one occasion or over a period of time, and whether intended for aggregate use by one or more individuals or for separate use by the individual members of a group; or

(2) engages in the systematic reproduction or distribution of single or multiple copies or phonorecords of material described in subsection (d): *Provided,* That nothing in this clause prevents a library or archives from participating in interlibrary arrangements that do not have, as their purpose or effect, that the library or archives receiving such copies or phonorecords for distribution does so in such aggregate quantities as to substitute for a subscription to or purchase of such work.

(h)(1) For purposes of this section, during the last 20 years of any term of copyright of a published work, a library or archives, including a nonprofit educational institution that functions as such, may reproduce, distribute, display, or perform in facsimile or digital form a copy or phonorecord of such work, or portions thereof, for purposes of preservation, scholarship, or research, if such library or archives has first determined, on the basis of a reasonable investigation, that none of the conditions set forth in subparagraphs (A), (B), and (C) of paragraph (2) apply.

(2) No reproduction, distribution, display, or performance is authorized under this subsection if—

(A) the work is subject to normal commercial exploitation;

(B) a copy or phonorecord of the work can be obtained at a reasonable price; or

(C) the copyright owner or its agent provides notice pursuant to regulations promulgated by the Register of Copyrights that either of the conditions set forth in subparagraphs (A) and (B) applies.

(3) The exemption provided in this subsection does not apply to any subsequent uses by users other than such library or archives.

(i) The rights of reproduction and distribution under this section do not apply to a musical work, a pictorial, graphic or sculptural work, or a motion picture or other audiovisual work other than an audiovisual work dealing with news, except that no such limitation shall apply with respect to rights granted by subsections (b) and (c), or with respect to pictorial or graphic works published as illustrations, diagrams, or similar adjuncts to works of which copies are reproduced or distributed in accordance with subsections (d) and (e).

Appendix A6
§ 110. Limitations on Exclusive Rights: Exemption of Certain Performances and Displays

Notwithstanding the provisions of section 106, the following are not infringements of copyright:

(1) performance or display of a work by instructors or pupils in the course of face-to-face teaching activities of a nonprofit educational institution, in a classroom or similar place devoted to instruction, unless, in the case of a motion picture or other audiovisual work, the performance, or the display of individual images, is given by means of a copy that was not lawfully made under this title, and that the person responsible for the performance knew or had reason to believe was not lawfully made;

(2) performance of a nondramatic literary or musical work or display of a work, by or in the course of a transmission, if—

(A) the performance or display is a regular part of the systematic instructional activities of a governmental body or a nonprofit educational institution; and

(B) the performance or display is directly related and of material assistance to the teaching content of the transmission; and

(C) the transmission is made primarily for —

(i) reception in classrooms or similar places normally devoted to instruction, or

(ii) reception by persons to whom the transmission is directed because their disabilities or other special circumstances prevent their attendance in classrooms or similar places normally devoted to instruction, or

(iii) reception by officers or employees of governmental bodies as a part of their official duties or employment;

[Other provisions of Section 110, not directly relevant to education, are omitted.]

Appendix A7
§ 504. Remedies for Infringement: Damages and Profits

(a) IN GENERAL.—Except as otherwise provided by this title, an infringer of copyright is liable for either —

(1) the copyright owner's actual damages and any additional profits of the infringer, as provided by subsection (b); or

(2) statutory damages, as provided by subsection (c).

(b) ACTUAL DAMAGES AND PROFITS.—The copyright owner is entitled to recover the actual damages suffered by him or her as a result of the infringement, and any profits of the infringer that are attributable to the infringement and are not taken into account in computing the actual damages. In establishing the infringer's profits, the copyright owner is required to present proof only of the infringer's gross revenue, and the infringer is required to prove his or her deductible expenses and the elements of profit attributable to factors other than the copyrighted work.

(c) STATUTORY DAMAGES.—

(1) Except as provided by clause (2) of this subsection, the copyright owner may elect, at any time before final judgment is rendered, to recover, instead of actual damages and profits, an award of statutory damages for all infringements involved in the action, with respect to any one work, for which any one infringer is liable individually, or for which any two or more infringers are liable jointly and severally, in a sum of not less than $750 or more than $30,000 as the court considers just. For the purposes of this subsection, all the parts of a compilation or derivative work constitute one work.

(2) In a case where the copyright owner sustains the burden of proving, and

the court finds, that infringement was committed willfully, the court in its discretion may increase the award of statutory damages to a sum of not more than $150,000. In a case where the infringer sustains the burden of proving, and the court finds, that such infringer was not aware and had no reason to believe that his or her acts constituted an infringement of copyright, the court in its discretion may reduce the award of statutory damages to a sum of not less than $200. The court shall remit statutory damages in any case where an infringer believed and had reasonable grounds for believing that his or her use of the copyrighted work was a fair use under section 107, if the infringer was: (i) an employee or agent of a nonprofit educational institution, library, or archives acting within the scope of his or her employment who, or such institution, library, or archives itself, which infringed by reproducing the work in copies or phonorecords; or (ii) a public broadcasting entity which or a person who, as a regular part of the nonprofit activities of a public broadcasting entity (as defined in subsection (g) of section 118) infringed by performing a published nondramatic literary work or by reproducing a transmission program embodying a performance of such a work.

(d) ADDITIONAL DAMAGES IN CERTAIN CASES. —In any case in which the court finds that a defendant proprietor of an establishment who claims as a defense that its activities were exempt under section 110(5) did not have reasonable grounds to believe that its use of a copyrighted work was exempt under such section, the plaintiff shall be entitled to, in addition to any award of damages under this section, an additional award of two times the amount of the license fee that the proprietor of the establishment concerned should have paid the plaintiff for such use during the preceding period of up to 3 years.

Appendix B

Summary of the
Digital Millennium Copyright Act

In the waning days of the 105th Congress, both the Senate and the House of Representatives overwhelmingly accepted a final version of the Digital Millennium Copyright Act (DMCA); the president signed it into law on October 28, 1998. The DMCA is lengthy and complex legislation that could revise the terms on which faculty, librarians, students, and staff may use email, websites, and other technology in libraries and for education. The new law could alter fundamental activities such as library services, research, website development, distance education, and Internet access. Much of this legislation has been highly controversial. Many educators and librarians had sought to prevent passage of the DMCA or had argued for revising many of its provisions to better foster innovative teaching and research. Some of those efforts were successful, leaving the final bill more acceptable than it might otherwise have been. In the final analysis, the DMCA affords some benefits for teaching and research, but overall it imposes enormous challenges.

This report summarizes the most salient provisions of the DMCA affecting libraries and education, and it suggests how the Act may require some changes in common practices. The Act is divided into "titles," and the organization of this summary reflects those title numbers.

Title I: WIPO Copyright Treaties Implementation

1. New Prohibitions on Using Copyrighted Works. This provision prohibits anyone from circumventing a "technological measure" that controls access to copyrighted works and prohibits removal of "copyright management information" from any work under many circumstances. For example, any action that bypasses computer restrictions on access to databases could become a violation of federal law. Moreover, removing a copyright notice or removing the names of authors from any work also could be a violation if the removal concealed or allowed an infringement of copyright to that work. Fundamentally, these provisions allow copyright owners to impose technological controls and other restrictions on the use of their works, and in the process, to constrain the use of materials for research and teaching in a manner more restrictive than may be established under existing copyright law. The copyright owner could conceivably impose conditions or fees for each use of any "technologically protected" works acquired by a library or educator.

2. Exceptions for the Benefit of Education and Libraries. These new restrictions are subject to several complex exceptions, many of which are specifically for the benefit of higher education. First, the prohibition on circumventing technological restrictions does not take effect until October 28, 2000. Second, once taking effect, the restrictions may not apply to particular classes of works and to particular persons, if the restrictions would "adversely affect" the ability to make "noninfringing uses" of those works, as determined by the U.S. Copyright Office. Further, libraries will be allowed to circumvent protections if they are reviewing the work in good faith for purposes of determining whether to purchase it. Moreover, the DMCA specifies that nothing in it will affect rights of fair use. Thus, while this new law imposes a heightened responsibility on educators and librarians to respect the rights of copyright owners, it would, in an awkward twist, allow breaking restrictive codes that may block otherwise lawful uses of copyrighted works. In order to implement such exceptions, individuals may need to review and determine the appropriateness of potentially technical activity; in order to manage the implications of this new law, libraries and universities may need to negotiate more aggressively with copyright owners to obtain more workable terms and fewer restrictions on protected materials.

3. Three-Year Review of the Law. During the initial two years after enactment, and every three years thereafter, the Librarian of Congress, upon recommendation of the Register of Copyrights, is required to conduct proceedings to examine and review the effect of the restrictions on the availability and use of copyrighted works, especially for education and libraries. These reviews are an opportunity to collect and present data and examples of these effects; they could also be the foundation of a major research study that could have national implications.

4. Encryption Research and Reverse Engineering. Researchers in these areas often need to circumvent technological controls in order to reverse engineer software or to undertake encryption research for the purpose of testing and improving the effectiveness of such controls. The DMCA allows continuance of those activities, but only under tightly defined circumstances. Accordingly, libraries and universities may need to monitor the reverse engineering of software, perhaps by prior approval from supervisors or other officials. A university may also need to subject any encryption research to advance review and approval, perhaps in a manner similar to current review of human-subjects studies.

Title II: Online Service Provider Liability

Reduced Risk of Infringement Liability for Computer Networks. In an important development for all institutions that provide Internet access, the DMCA potentially eliminates some risks of copyright infringement liability for an online-service provider ("OSP"), subject to numerous conditions specified in the Act. An OSP is defined broadly as "an entity offering the transmission, routing, or providing of connections for digital online communications." Many educational institutions routinely offer these services to faculty, librarians, staff, and the broader community. Possible infringements may occur when a user of the network or system transmits copyrighted works, caches works in computer memory, includes a work on a website, or possibly even links to an infringing work on another site. The service provider may be able to escape liability for infringements committed by faculty and other users, generally if it is acting solely as a conduit for the transmission of information. The liability, however, remains with the individual who committed the infringement.

The DMCA might provide a welcome degree of legal certainty about potential OSP liability, but that benefit comes at a significant price. The new law requires implementation of numerous operational procedures that, if not carefully applied and monitored, could sharply limit the use of technologies for teaching and research, and that could raise serious problems of academic freedom and appropriate oversight of faculty activities and discipline for malfeasance.

In general, the university may escape liability upon meeting elaborate, technical conditions related to the structure of the network system. In addition, the university must meet numerous procedural conditions, such as the following:

- Designating an agent who would receive notifications of claimed infringements submitted by third parties. The U.S. Copyright Office would record this information and provide a publicly available directory of such agents, assessing a fee for this service.
- Implementing, administering, and tracking notifications of claimed infringements committed by users of the system and expeditiously removing or disabling access to material.
- Adopting a policy and informing subscribers and account holders of the policy that would provide for termination of service if that subscriber or account holder repeatedly infringes the copyrights of third parties.
- Removing or disabling access to materials if the service provider obtains knowledge of infringing activity or becomes aware of facts that suggest infringement.
- Adhering to numerous and extensive technical requirements for the storage and transmission of the infringing materials and all materials that may be communicated on the OSP's system or network.

Under well-established law, an employer is ordinarily likely to be liable for the unlawful activities of employees acting within their duties at the workplace. Thus, if a university provides email and website services to faculty members for their teaching and research, the university may not be acting as a "mere conduit" for the communication, as would a typical OSP. Instead, the university may be liable as would any other employer. The DMCA extends the OSP protection to such a university, even in the context of faculty activities, but subject to additional conditions:

- The OSP is a public or nonprofit educational institution.
- The claimed infringements are made by a "faculty member or graduate student who is an employee" of the university and who is "performing a teaching or research function."
- The infringing activities do not involve providing online access to "required or recommended" instructional materials.
- The university has not received more than two formal notices of claimed infringement during the preceding three years with respect to that faculty member or graduate student. While the statute disqualifies notices that make "intentionally" false claims, the law does not deal with the problem of notices that may inadvertently prove to be false, incorrect, or otherwise not claiming an actual infringement due to fair use or other legal exception.
- The university provides "all users of its system or network" information about copyright, and that information must "accurately describe, and promote compliance with, the laws of the United States relating to copyright."

Needless to say, these additional requirements are onerous. Together with a requirement to remove or disable access to the materials "expeditiously" upon notification, these conditions on the use of technology for teaching and research pose serious practical and legal problems for the university that may be seeking to enjoy the limited benefits of the OSP protection. Logistically, an OSP is expected to implement numerous administrative processes, beginning with appointment of a "designated agent" to receive claims of infringement and to institute the process of removing materials from the network. Further, the process of notification of claimed infringements, the rigid opportunity for the individual to justify the activity as fair use or as otherwise permitted under the law, the OSP's commitment to remove the material, and the OSP's obligation to terminate email and website privileges for some faculty, may also result in violations of academic freedom and constitutional principles of due process and free speech, if they are not handled in a cautious manner.

In exchange for meeting these conditions, the OSP receives limited protection. It is protected from liability arising only from the copyright infringements, but not arising from other legal claims that may even arise from the same activity, such as breach of contract, trademark infringement, or defamation.

Title IVB: Additional Provisions of Importance to Librarians and Educators

1. Possible Revision of the Law for Distance Education. The DMCA charges the Copyright Office with the duty to recommend to Congress any changes in the law with respect to the use of copyrighted works in distance education. Given the growth of these activities at many colleges and universities, this provision is of tremendous importance. Existing "distance-education" law, Section 110(2) of the Copyright Act, sets sharp restrictions on the use of materials in distance education. The potential magnitude of the Copyright Office study is enormous, because "distance education" today encompasses multiple forms of transmission, from television to websites, and includes the vast range of copyrighted materials, from text to software, that enhance the educational experience. The DMCA calls into consideration the teaching content permitted in distance education, the likely need for consistent controls on access and delivery, and the availability of licensing for the use of copyrighted works. The Copyright Office reported its findings and recommendations to Congress in May 1999. Those findings and recommendations may have momentous consequences for all colleges and universities.

2. Library Copying and Preservation. The amendments to Section 108 of the Copyright Act offer good and bad news for libraries. First, they clarify and assure that preservation copies of unique or deteriorating works may be made in digital formats; however, the digital version may be used only on the library premises. Second, they allow the library to copy works if the works are currently in formats that have become technologically obsolete. Finally, the amendments address a long-standing controversy in Section 108 by specifying that all copies made by the library under Section 108 must include the formal copyright notice, if available, or a specified statement about the applicability of copyright to the work.

A version of this document was originally prepared for the Indiana University community by the Copyright Management Center. It is the work of Dwayne K. Buttler, Senior Copyright Analyst of the CMC; Noemí Rivera-Morales, graduate student in the IU School of Library and Information Science; and Prof. Kenneth Crews; it is available from <http://www.iupui.edu/~copyinfo/dmcamemo.html>.

Appendix C

Summary of the U.S. Copyright Office Report on Distance Education

A new report from the U.S. Copyright Office addresses many of the difficult issues surrounding the use of copyrighted works in distance education (full text of this report is available from <www.loc.gov/copyright/docs/de_rprt.pdf>). The Copyright Office also has proposed revisions to the law that would achieve a more meaningful and workable balance between the rights of copyright owners and users, while promoting the continued growth of distance education using digital technologies. Should Congress enact those proposals, educators would have new options for including some copyrighted works in transmissions to students at remote locations. In addition, educators would need to limit access to students enrolled in the course, implement systems for informing students and others about copyright, and strive to prevent misuse of copyrighted content by students through education programs and warning notices.

The Copyright Office report responds directly to the many serious problems with adapting existing law for distance education to modern technologies. Educational programs regularly involve the use of text, video, music, images, and other copyrighted works. If the instructor is not the copyright owner of the individual works, or does not have permission from the copyright owner, many common uses of these works could be unlawful. The copyright owner generally holds rights of reproduction, distribution, display, and performance of copyrighted works. Thus, simply showing or playing works for students may be an infringing "display or performance." Sharing copies of the works, whether in analog format or through digital delivery of the course, could constitute an infringing "reproduction or distribution."

In order to foster quality education and to prevent these common educational uses from becoming violations, the law long has allowed instructors to make displays and performances of works in the live, face-to-face classroom at nonprofit educational institutions. (Note that this broad right of use is limited to face-to-face teaching and covers only performances and displays; it does not cover the ability to make copies of works.) Once the educational experience is "transmitted" to remote locations, however, existing law, enacted by Congress in 1976, sets rigorous ground rules and applies sharp limits on the types of works that may be used at all.

Existing law poses serious problems for the effective development of distance education. It generally restricts delivery of the course to students who are located in classrooms or other similar locations. Even then, the course content may not include audiovisual works and "dramatic" literary and musical works. Clearly, the law does not foster the growth of distance learning through digital technologies, where students may access works at diverse locations other than a "classroom," and where the transmission necessarily involves some incidental copies in order to make the display or performance of a work possible. Moreover, the disallowance of whole categories of works forces illogical barriers on the advancement of learning.

In October 1998, Congress charged the Copyright Office with the duty of examining the issues and making recommendations. While delivery of the report was delayed slightly, the result is an ambitious study that surveys problems with existing law, identifies the underlying policies for striking a balance between protecting the rights of copyright owners, and articulates promising solutions that would allow educators to use works under limited circumstances.

In the end, the report makes important and thoughtful recommendations for revising the statute. The following is a summary of those recommendations.

1. **Expand coverage of rights to meet technological necessities.** In particular, digital transmissions involve the making of incidental copies to make the transmission—or display and performance—possible. The Copyright Office is not suggesting that educators should be allowed to make copies of works for students in distance learning: "Rather, the amendment should include these rights only to the extent technologically required in order to transmit the performance or display authorized by the exemption." Specifically, the Copyright Office is contemplating the "transient copies" that are "part of the automatic technical process" of the transmission.

2. **Allow displays and performances in the context of "mediated instruction."** The Copyright Office identified concerns with the prospect of "electronic reserves" or other arrangements whereby entire works are made available to students, thus potentially substituting for sales of those works. To facilitate uses of works for educational purposes, however, the report recommends that works be used in a context where the instructor is illustrating a point or where the use is an integral part of a course structure.

3. **Expand the scope of allowed materials.** The recommendations would eliminate the current proscription of "dramatic" works and audiovisual works. On the other hand, the proposal would allow only "limited portions" of those works in a manner consistent with the "nature of the market for that type of work and the pedagogical purposes of the use." For example, an instructor could use "the equivalent of a film clip, rather than a substantial part of the film." This approach appears consistent with the recommendation that the

materials be used in the context of "mediated instruction," during which only portions may typically be needed for discussion and analysis. Whole works may, of course, be available to students in the library, at reserve desks, or in the bookstore. They may also be placed on a Web-delivery system with permission from the copyright owner.

4. **Eliminate the requirement of transmitting the educational experience solely to classrooms and similar places.** The Copyright Office is recommending that Congress allow educators to transmit the content of distance-education courses to enrolled students, regardless of their physical location.

5. **Implement safeguards to reduce risks to the copyright owners.** First, the transient copies that result from the digital transmission may be retained only as needed to complete the transmission. Second, the institution must develop policies that describe copyright law and must provide those policies to students, faculty, and others. Third, the transmission to students must include a notice that the content of the transmission may be subject to copyright protection. Fourth, the institution should implement technological protections that reasonably prevent unauthorized access and further dissemination of the material.

6. **Allow retention of a copy of the distance-education program on a server for access limited to students in the course during the duration of the course.** Students would therefore be able to review earlier materials and vary their pace of learning. That copy would be retained by the institution, and no further copies would be allowed.

7. **Continue to apply fair use to activities outside the exemption for distance education.** Examples of possible fair use include: converting a work from analog to digital format for transmission, and using no more than a "limited portion" of a work. The report also emphasizes that "guidelines" interpreting fair use are not the law and may at best provide a "safe harbor" from potential liability. Although the Copyright Office appears critical of the effort to develop guidelines in the recently concluded "Conference on Fair Use," the Copyright Office remains hopeful that future understandings of fair use may emerge from discussions among diverse stakeholders.

What do these developments mean for educational institutions? In the short run, the issuance of the report draws attention to serious deficiencies in current law. Before rushing to implement changes, however, educators should recognize that the report from the Copyright Office includes only *recommendations*. Proposals cannot become law until Congress enacts them in legislation. Educators may review the proposals from the U.S. Copyright Office and contact members of Congress with their statements of support or concern.

Should these recommendations become law, educational institutions will need to take important steps to expand educational opportunities and to protect the interests of copyright owners. Some of those steps could include:

1. Inform faculty members of limits on the use of works in distance education. Given the importance of academic freedom in planning courses, the university is not likely to review individual course content. Instead, the university may prefer to inform educators about the copyright implications of their work and offer standards for appropriate course planning. The university may accomplish that goal through the distribution of literature or by sponsoring seminars or workshops for instructors.

2. Develop a policy that describes and explains relevant copyright law, and assure that the policy is disseminated widely to all faculty and students.

3. Include a warning statement about copyright on the "front page" of all distance-education transmissions.

4. Retain all distance-education courses on university-owned servers or other delivery equipment.

5. Assure that only enrolled students are able to access the transmission.

6. Preserve technological devices or systems that copyright owners may use to limit misuse of their works, when those works are used in distance education.

7. Prepare to address the applicability of "fair use" to activities, such as electronic reserves, that are not specifically addressed by the exemption for distance education.

An earlier version of this document is available from <http://www.iupui.edu/~copyinfo/distedsum.html>.

Appendix D

Copyright Notices for Supervised Library Copying: Updated Information for Library Services

Section 108 of the U.S. Copyright Act allows qualifying libraries to make limited copies of materials under specific conditions. In general, libraries may make copies for preservation, for replacement of lost, damaged, or stolen works, for upgrading to some new formats, for private research and study by library users, and for delivery to other libraries through interlibrary loan (the full text of Section 108 is available from <http://www.iupui.edu/~copyinfo/sec108.html>). This overview focuses on the notices that libraries are required to post whenever staff members make copies for library patrons. Portions of this overview reflect procedures that have been part of the law since its most recent full revision in 1976; other portions reflect changes in the law made by the Digital Millennium Copyright Act, passed by Congress in October 1998.

Section 108 requires that supervised copying services in libraries employ two notices: (1) an advisory notice posted at the place where requests are made and on order forms that patrons may fill out to request copies; and (2) a notice of copyright on the copies themselves.

Notice at Order Desk and on Order Forms

The law prescribes the form of notice that must be posted at the desk where orders for copies are accepted and on order forms:

NOTICE: WARNING CONCERNING COPYRIGHT RESTRICTIONS

The copyright law of the United States (Title 17, United States Code) governs the making of photocopies or other reproductions of copyrighted material.

Under certain conditions specified in the law, libraries and archives are authorized to furnish a photocopy or other reproduction. One of these specific conditions is that the photocopy or reproduction is not to be

"used for any purpose other than private study, scholarship, or research."
If a user makes a request for, or later uses, a photocopy or reproduction
for purposes in excess of "fair use," that user may be liable for copyright
infringement.

This institution reserves the right to refuse a copying order if, in its judg-
ment, fulfillment of the order would involve violation of copyright law.

According to regulations from the U.S. Copyright Office (Code of Federal Regulations, Title 37, Section 201.14), this warning must be displayed verbatim and "printed on heavy paper or other durable material in type at least 18 points in size, and shall be displayed prominently in such manner and location as to be clearly visible, legible, and comprehensible to a casual observer within the immediate vicinity of the place where orders are accepted."

When printing this notice on order forms, the regulations specify that it: "shall be printed within a box located prominently on the order form itself, either on the front side of the form or immediately adjacent to the space calling for the name or signature of the person using the form. The notice shall be printed in type size no smaller than that used predominantly throughout the form, and in no case shall the type size be smaller than 8 points. The notice shall be printed in such manner as to be clearly legible, comprehensible, and readily apparent to a casual reader of the form."

Notices on Copies

The law also requires that the copies themselves include a notice, but the law does not specify the exact form of that notice. For more than twenty years, librarians and publishers debated whether the "notice" on the copy should be the formal copyright notice as found on the original (for example, "Copyright 1999, XYZ Publishing Company"), or whether it need only be some general indication that copyright applied to the work (for example, "use of this material is governed by copyright law"). The Digital Millennium Copyright Act resolved that debate. All copies made under Section 108 now must include the notice of copyright as it appears on the original work. If no notice appears on the original, then the copy must include "a legend stating that the work may be protected by copyright."

Accordingly, the Copyright Management Center suggests that libraries making copies pursuant to Section 108 adopt and implement the following procedures with respect to all copies.

1. If the original work includes a formal copyright notice, the copy should include the following statement: *"The work from which this copy was made included the following copyright notice: _____."*

The librarian making the copy should transcribe the original copyright notice into the blank space. When making a copy of a work, many librarians instead routinely photocopy the page from the book or journal on which the copyright notice appears. Attaching a photocopy of the original notice to the copied article ought to be satisfactory.

2. If the version of the work available to the librarian making the copy does not include a formal copyright notice, the librarian must place on the copy "a legend stating that the work may be protected by copyright." Such a "legend" may take many forms, but the following form may be helpful to librarians and patrons:

   The work from which this copy was made did not include a formal copyright notice. This work may be protected under U.S. Copyright Law (Title 17, U.S. Code), which governs reproduction, distribution, public display, and certain other uses of protected works. Uses may be allowed with permission from the rightsholder, or if the copyright on the work has expired, or if the use is "fair use" or within another exemption. The user of this work is responsible for determining lawful uses.

In an effort to be helpful, this suggested form of notices includes more information than the law actually requires. If your objective is only to comply with the law, consider using this statement: "This material may be protected by copyright." If the user of the copy may need to trace the copy to the originating library (as may be the case with manuscripts secured from the collections of archives or special collections), the library may want to include with that notice a simple statement such as: "IUPUI University Library, Special Collections and Archives (317) _____."

Appendix E

Checklist for Fair Use:
Introduction

We are pleased to offer the following "Checklist for Fair Use" as a helpful tool for the academic community. We hope that it will serve two purposes. First, it should help educators, librarians, and others to focus on factual circumstances that are important to the evaluation of a contemplated fair use of copyrighted works. A reasonable fair-use analysis is based on four factors set forth in the fair-use provision of copyright law: Section 107 of the Copyright Act of 1976. The application of those factors depends on the particular facts of your situation, and changing one or more facts may alter the outcome of the analysis. The "checklist for fair use" derives from those four factors and from the judicial decisions interpreting copyright law.

For additional information about fair use and its application to the needs of education, read the following publications from the Copyright Management Center:

- *Fair Use: Overview and Meaning for Higher Education*, Kenneth D. Crews (available from <http://www.iupui.edu/~copyinfo/highered2000.html>).
- *A Fair-Use Case Study: Using Copyrighted Materials on the World Wide Web*, Dwayne K. Buttler (available from <http://www.iupui.edu/~copyinfo/fucasestudy.html>).

A second purpose of the checklist is to provide an important means for recording your decision-making process. Maintaining a record of your fair-use analysis is critical to establishing your "reasonable and good-faith" attempts to apply fair use to meet your educational objectives. The Indiana University Policy on Fair Use of Copyrighted Works for Education and Research requires reasonable and good-faith applications of fair use from all members of the university community. Once you have completed your application of fair use to a particular need, keep your completed checklist in your files for future reference.

As you use the checklist and apply it to your situation, you are likely to check more than one box in each column and even check boxes across columns. Some checked boxes will "favor fair use," and others may "oppose fair use." A key concern is whether you are acting reasonably in checking any given box; the ultimate concern is whether the cumulative "weight" of the factors favors or opposes fair use. Only you can make that decision, and the IU policy empowers you to make it in a reasonable and good-faith manner.

To learn more about fair use and other aspects of copyright law, visit the Copyright Management Center website at http://www.iupui.edu/~copyinfo.

CHECKLIST FOR FAIR USE

Please complete and retain a copy of this form in connection with each possible "fair use" of a copyrighted work for your project

Name:_____   Date:_____

Institution:_____   Project:_____

PURPOSE

Favoring Fair Use	*Opposing Fair Use*
❑ Teaching (including multiple copies for classroom use)	❑ Commercial activity
❑ Research	❑ Profiting from the use
❑ Scholarship	❑ Entertainment
❑ Nonprofit Educational Institution	❑ Bad-faith behavior
❑ Criticism	❑ Denying credit to original author
❑ Comment	
❑ News reporting	
❑ Transformative or Productive use (changes the work for new utility)	
❑ Restricted access (to students or other appropriate group)	
❑ Parody	

NATURE

Favoring Fair Use	*Opposing Fair Use*
❑ Published work	❑ Unpublished work
❑ Factual or nonfiction based	❑ Highly creative work (art, music, novels, films, plays)
❑ Important to favored educational objectives	❑ Fiction

AMOUNT

Favoring Fair Use	*Opposing Fair Use*
❑ Small quantity	❑ Large portion or whole work used
❑ Portion used is not central or significant to entire work	❑ Portion used is central to work or "heart of the work"
❑ Amount is appropriate for favored educational purpose	

EFFECT

Favoring Fair Use	*Opposing Fair Use*
❑ User owns lawfully acquired or purchased copy of original work	❑ Could replace sale of copyrighted work
❑ One or few copies made	❑ Significantly impairs market or potential market for copyrighted work or derivative
❑ No significant effect on the market or potential market for copyrighted work	❑ Reasonably available licensing mechanism for use of the copyrighted work
❑ No similar product marketed by the copyright holder	❑ Affordable permission available for using work
❑ Lack of licensing mechanism	❑ Numerous copies made
	❑ You made it accessible on Web or in other public forum
	❑ Repeated or long-term use

Appendix F

Supplemental Reading List, 1998-2000

Chapters 1-2
Copyright in General

Alpern, Andrew. *101 Questions about Copyright Law*. Mineola, NY: Dover Publications, 1999.

Elias, Stephen. *Patent, Copyright & Trademark: A Desk Reference to Intellectual Property Law*. 3d ed. Berkeley: Nolo Press, 1999.

Fishman, Stephen. *The Copyright Handbook: How to Protect & Use Written Works*. 5th ed. Berkeley: Nolo Press, 1999.

Jasper, Margaret C. *The Law of Copyright*. Legal Almanac Series: Law for the Layperson. Dobbs Ferry, NY: Oceana Publications, 1999.

Leaffer, Marshall A. *Understanding Copyright Law*. 3d ed. New York: Matthew Bender, 1999.

National Research Council, Committee on Intellectual Property Rights and the Emerging Information Infrastructure. *The Digital Dilemma: Intellectual Property in the Information Age*. Washington, D.C.: National Academy Press, 2000.

Perle, E. Gabriel, et al. *Perle and Williams on Publishing Law*. Rev. ed. Gaithersburg, MD: Aspen Law and Business, 1999.

Strong, William S. *The Copyright Book: A Practical Guide*. 5th ed. Cambridge, MA: MIT Press, 1999.

Talab, R. S. *Commonsense Copyright: A Guide for Educators and Librarians*. Jefferson, NC: McFarland, 1999.

Chapters 3-5
Scope of Protectable Works

Bernstein, Robert J. and Robert W. Clarida. "Art Reproductions: What's Wrong with this Picture?" *New York Law Journal* 221 (March 19, 1999): 3.

Halpin, Jon. "When Freedom Hurts: Copyright Protection of Internet Content and Digital Rights Management." *Computer Shopper* 19 (June 1999): 262.

Hoffman, Barbara. "Protecting Art Images: Whether a Museum or Archive Owns Reproductions Depends on the Originality Involved." *National Law Journal* 22 (October 25, 1999): C1.

Chapters 6-7
Works Not Protectable under Copyright

Hatmaker, Scott. "Government Information: Public Domain or User Beware?" *Information Outlook* 1 (December 1997): 39.

Silverman, Arnold B. "Congress Eyes Bills Protecting Databases." *Intellectual Property Today* 6 (November 1999): 46.

Wiant, Sarah K. "Copyright and Government Libraries." *Information Outlook* 3 (February 1999): 38-39.

Chapters 8-9
Formalities of Copyright

Gardner, Elizabeth. "Filing a Copyright to Protect Online Content Is Not So Easy." *Internet World* 5 (May 10, 1999): 19.

U.S. Copyright Office. *Copyright Registration for Computer Programs*. Circular 61. Washington, D.C.: Library of Congress, 1999.

————. *Copyright Registration for Derivative Works*. Circular 14. Washington, D.C.: Library of Congress, 1999.

————. *Copyright Registration for Multimedia Works*. Circular 55. Washington, D.C.: Library of Congress, 1999.

————. *Copyright Registration for Online Works*. Circular 66. Washington, D.C.: Library of Congress, 1999.

—————. *Copyright Registration for Works of the Visual Arts*. Circular 40. Washington, D.C.: Library of Congress, 1999.

Chapters 10-11
Duration of Copyright

Bard, Robert L. and Lewis S. Kurlantzick. *Copyright Duration: Duration, Term Extension, the European Union and the Making of Copyright Policy*. San Francisco: Austin and Winfield, 1999.

Fishman, Stephen. *The Public Domain: How to Find and Use Copyright-Free Writings, Music, Art, and More*. Berkeley: Nolo.com., 2000.

Lewis, Paul. "The Artist's Friend Turned Enemy: A Backlash against the Copyright." *New York Times*, January 8, 2000, p. 9.

Potter, Kenyon David. *An Educator's Guide to Finding Resources in the Public Domain*. Bloomington, IN: Phi Delta Kappa Educational Foundation, 1999.

Young, Jeffrey R. "An On-line Publisher Files Court Challenge to Copyright Extension Law." *Chronicle of Higher Education* 45 (January 22, 1999): A20.

Zimmerman, Barbara. *The Mini-Encyclopedia of Public Domain Songs*. New York: BZ Rights Stuff, 1999.

Chapters 12-14
Ownership of Copyright

Carnevale, Dan and Jeffrey R. Young. "Who Owns On-Line Courses?: Colleges and Professors Start to Sort It Out." *Chronicle of Higher Education* 46 (December 17, 1999): A45.

Chambers, Gail S. "Toward Shared Control of Distance Education." *Chronicle of Higher Education* 46 (November 19, 1999): B8.

Fitzgerald, Clare Anne. "Freelance Journalism after *Tasini*." *Legal Intelligencer*, February 2, 2000, p. 5.

Harvard Law Review Association. "Second Circuit Holds that Dramaturg's Contributions to the Musical *Rent* Did Not Establish Joint Authorship with Playwright-Composer." *Harvard Law Review* 112 (February 1999): 964-69.

Holmes, Georgia and Daniel A. Levin. "Who Owns Course Materials Prepared by a Teacher or Professor? The Application of Copyright Law to Teaching Materials in the Internet Age." *Brigham Young University Education and Law Journal* (2000): 165-89.

Marcus, Amy Dockser. "Seeing Crimson: Why Harvard Law Wants to Rein in One of Its Star Professors." *Wall Street Journal*, November 22, 1999, p. A1.

Martinez, Frank. "Owning Up." *Print* 53 (May-June 1999): 28.

McKinnon, John D. "Florida Journal: University's Cyber Class Spark Faculty Concerns." *Wall Street Journal*, July 15, 1998, p. F1.

Oder, Norman. "Freelancers Win Copyright Suit." *Library Journal* 124 (October 15, 1999): 18.

Young, Jeffrey R. "A Debate over Ownership of On-line Courses Surfaces at Drexel U." *Chronicle of Higher Education* 45 (April 9, 1999): A31.

Chapter 15
Rights of Copyright Owners

Band, Jonathan. *The Digital Millennium Copyright Act*. Washington, D.C.: Association of Research Libraries, October 20, 1998. Available from <http://www.arl.org/info/frn/copy/band.html>.

Camber, Rachel A. "A Visual Art Law You Had Better Not Overlook." *Florida Bar Journal* 73 (May 1999): 69.

Gasaway, Laura N. "Digital Millennium Copyright Act: A Mixed Bag." *Information Outlook* 3 (March 1999): 14.

Gendreau, Ysolde, ed. *Copyright and Photographs: An International Survey*. Information Law Series 7. Boston: Kluwer Law International, 1999.

Hoffman, Barbara, ed. *Exploiting Images and Image Collections in the New Media–Gold Mine or Legal Minefield?* Cambridge, MA: Kluwer Law International, 1999.

Lutzker, Arnold P., et al. *The Digital Millennium Copyright Act: Highlights of New Copyright Provision Establishing Limitation of Liability for Online Service Providers*. Washington, D.C.: Association of Research Libraries, November 12, 1998. Available from <http://www.arl.org/info/frn/copy/osp.html>.

Rosenbaum, David G. *Patents, Trademarks, and Copyrights: Practical Legal Strategies for Protecting Your Ideas and Inventions*. 3d ed. Franklin Lakes, NJ: Career; Biblios, 1999.

Chapter 16
Rights of Copyright Owners: Reproduction and Distribution

"Digital Copyright Protection: Good or Bad for Libraries?" *Information Outlook* 3 (January 1999): 32.

"Digitisation: Steps out of Copyright 'Hit-and-Miss.'" *Library Association Record* 101 (June 1999): 327.

Chapter 17
Rights of Copyright Owners: Derivative Works

Harvard Law Review Association. "Seventh Circuit Holds that Mounting Copyrighted Notecards on Ceramic Tiles Does Not Constitute Preparation of Derivative Works in Violation of the Copyright Act." *Harvard Law Review* 111 (March 1998): 1365-70.

Oberman, Michael S. and Alan Behr. "Protecting a Valuable IP Franchise: The Copyright Solution." *Intellectual Property Today* 6 (May 1999): 44.

Vitanza, Elisa. Comment. "*Castle Rock Entertainment, Inc. v. Carol Publishing Group, Inc.*" *Berkeley Technology Law Journal* 14 (Winter 1999): 43.

Chapter 18
Rights of Copyright Owners: Performances and Displays

Cochran, J. Wesley. "Using Copyrighted Works for Meetings, Seminars, and Conferences." *Information Outlook* 3 (July 1999): 42.

Shapiro, Michael Steven and Brett I. Miller. *A Museum Guide to Copyright and Trademark*. Washington, DC: American Association of Museums, 1999.

Wienand, Peter. *A Guide to Copyright for Museums and Galleries*. New York: Routledge, 2000.

Chapters 20-27
Fair Use

Hartnick, Alan J. "ABC's of 'Fair Use.'" *New York Law Journal*, November 8, 1999, p. 3.

Nag, Rupak. "Parody or Parasite? A Copyright Fair Use Analysis." *Intellectual Property Today* 6 (February 1999): 36.

Kolhatkar, Sonali R. Comment. "Yesterday's Love Letters Are Today's Best Sellers: Fair Use & the War among Authors." *John Marshall Journal of Computer and Information Law* 18 (Fall 1999): 141-79.

Orlans, Harold. "Scholarly Fair Use." *Change* 31 (November 1999): 53.

Chapter 28
Fair Use on the Internet

Berthelsen, Christian. "Setback for a Web Site in Copyright Case." *New York Times*, November 15, 1999, p. C23.

Miller, Greg. "Judge Rejects 'Fair Use' of News Protection." *Los Angeles Times*, November 9, 1999, p. C-1.

Nimmer, David. "A Riff on Fair Use in the Digital Millennium Copyright Act." *University of Pennsylvania Law Review* 148 (January 2000): 673-742.

Ritter, Scott. "High Court Spurns Appeal of Man Who Violated Scientology Copyright Online." *Dow Jones Business News*, January 10, 2000, p. 1.

Chapters 29-30
Fair-Use Guidelines

Crews, Kenneth D. and Dwayne K. Buttler, eds. "Perspectives on Fair-Use Guidelines for Education and Libraries," *Journal of the American Society for Information Science* 51 (December 1999): 1303-57.

Galtin, Rebecca, et al. "AACSB Deans' Understanding of Multimedia Copyright Laws and Guidelines." *Journal of Education for Business* 74 (July 1999): 368-71.

Klingsporn, Gregory K. "The Conference on Fair Use (CONFU) and the Future of Fair Use Guidelines." *Columbia-VLA Journal of Law & Arts* 23 (Winter 1999): 101.

Marley, Judith L. "Guidelines Favoring Fair Use: An Analysis of Legal Interpretations Affecting Higher Education." *Journal of Academic Librarianship* 25 (September 1999): 367-71.

Chapter 31
Displays and Performances in Distance Learning

Council of the American Association of University Professors, Special Committee on Distance Education and Intellectual Property Issues. "Distance Education and Intellectual Property." *Academe* 85 (May-June 1999): 41-45.

Flower, Ruth. "The Scholar's Copyright." *Academe* 85 (July-August 1999): 69.

McCollum, Kelly. "Copyright Office Releases Proposal for On-line Distance Education." *Chronicle of Higher Education* 45 (June 18, 1999): A30.

Salomon, Kenneth D. "A Distance Education Exemption?" *Community College Journal* 70 (October-November 1999): 52-55.

Chapters 32-34
Library Copying

Ardito, Stephanie C., et al. "Realistic Approaches to Enigmatic Copyright Issues." *Online Magazine* 23 (May 1999): 91-92.

Connolly, P. "Interlending and Document Supply: A Review of Recent Literature." *Interlending and Document Supply* 27 (1999): 33-41.

Cornish, Graham P. *Copyright: Interpreting the Law for Libraries, Archives and Information Services*. London: Library Services, 1999.

Crosby, J. "Digital Copyright Protection: Good or Bad for Libraries?" *Information Outlook* 3 (January 1999): 32.

Eiblum, Paula and Stephanie C. Ardito. "Document Delivery & Copyright: Librarians Take the Fifth." *Online Magazine* 23 (September 1999): 73-76.

Friend, F. J. "Copyright: Will It Strangle Information?" In *Proceedings of the 24th Annual Conference of the International Association of Aquatic and Marine Science Libraries and Information Centers (IAMSLIC)*, James W. Markham, et al., eds., pp. 59-65. Fort Pierce, Florida: IAMSLIC, 1999.

Gasaway, Laura N. "Library Preservation and Recent Copyright Act Amendments." *Information Outlook* 3 (April 1999): 38.

Orlans, Harold. "Copyright Capers: Copying Alarm." *Change* 31 (July-August 1999): 6-7.

Ponis, Roberta. "Navigating the Muddy Waters of Copyright in School Libraries." *Colorado Libraries* 25 (Fall 1999): 24-26.

Chapter 35
Copyright and New Technology: Computer Software

Association for Computing Machinery (ACM). *Intellectual Property in the Age of Universal Access: A Collection of Articles from Leading Authorities Defines and Interprets the Emerging Technologies and the Laws They Instigate.* New York: ACM, 1999.

Bielefield, Arlene. *Technology and Copyright Law: A Guidebook for the Library, Research, and Teaching Professions: 1999 Update.* New York: Neal-Schuman Publishers, 1999.

Fishman, Stephen. *Software Development: A Legal Guide.* 2d ed. Berkeley: Nolo Press, 1999.

Graham, Lawrence D. *Legal Battles That Shaped the Computer Industry.* Westport, CT: Quorum, 1999.

Woo, Jisuk. *Copyright Law and Computer Programs: The Role of Communication in Legal Structure.* New York: Garland, 1999.

Chapter 36
Copyright and New Technology: The World Wide Web

Albert, G. Peter. *Intellectual Property Law in Cyberspace.* Washington, DC: Bureau of National Affairs, 1999.

Appel, Sharon E. "The Copyright Wars at the Digital Frontier: Which Side Are Art Museums On?" *Journal of Arts Management, Law and Society* 29 (Fall 1999): 205.

Bockanic, William N. and Patrick T. Hogan. "Legal Issues Involving the Operation of a University Web Site." *Journal of Education for Business* 74 (July 1999): 373-78.

Flower, Ruth. "The Scholar's Copyright." *Academe* 85 (July-August 1999): 69.

McCollum, Kelly and Peter Schmidt. "How Forcefully Should Universities Enforce Copyright Law on Audio Files?" *Chronicle of Higher Education* 46 (November 19, 1999): A59-60.

Oliva, Ralph A. and Sharda Prabakar. "Copyright Perils Can Lurk on the Business Web." *Marketing Management* 8 (Spring 1999): 54.

Peek, R. "Taming the Internet in Three Acts: The DMCA, ITFA, and COPA Have Far-Reaching Implications for the Web." *Information Today* 16 (January 1999): 28-29.

Pickering, Linda and Mauricio F. Paez. "Music on the Internet: How to Minimize Liability Risks While Benefiting from the Use of Music on the Internet." *Business Lawyer* 55 (November 1999): 409.

U.S. Copyright Office. *Digital Millennium Copyright Act of 1998: U.S. Copyright Office Summary*. Washington, D.C., December 1998. Available from <http://lcweb.loc.gov/copyright/legislation/dmca.pdf>.

Chapter 37
Requesting Permission from the Copyright Owner

Bielefield, Arlene. *Interpreting and Negotiating Licensing Agreements: A Guidebook for the Library, Research, and Teaching Professionals*. New York: Allworth Press, 1999.

Crawford, Tad. *Business and Legal Forms for Authors and Self-Publishers*. New York: Allworth Press, 1999.

Kohn, Al. *Kohn on Music Licensing*. 2d ed. Gaithersburg, MD: Aspen Law & Business, 1999.

Orlans, Harold. "Copyright Capers: Copying Alarm." *Change* 31 (July-August 1999): 6-7.

Port, Kenneth L., ed. *Licensing Intellectual Property in the Digital Age*. Durham, NC: Carolina Academic Press, 1999.

Sharp, Charles C. *Patent, Trademark, and Copyright Searching on the Internet*. Jefferson, NC: McFarland, 1999.

Stim, Richard. *Getting Permission: How to License & Clear Copyrighted Materials Online & Off*. Berkeley: Nolo Press, 1999.

Chapters 38-40
Liability and Infringement

Bray, Michael J., et al. "The World Wide Web and the New World of Litigation: A Basic Introduction." *Defense Counsel Journal* 66 (October 1999): 497.

McCollum, Kelly. "Student Gets 2 Years' Probation in Copyright Case." *Chronicle of Higher Education* 46 (December 10, 1999): A51.

Paradise, Paul R. *Trademark Counterfeiting, Product Piracy, and the Billion Dollar Threat to the U.S. Economy*. Westport, CT: Quorum, 1999.

Online Bibliographies

International Federation of Library Associations and Institutions, Information Policy: Copyright and Intellectual Property, at <http://www.ifla.org/II/cpyright.htm#bibliography>.

Missouri University Copyright Bibliography, at <http://web.missouri.edu/~engjudy/cpbibl.html>.

Rutgers University Copyright Resources, at <http://www.scils.rutgers.edu:80/special/kay/copyrightissues.html>.

Special Libraries Association, at <http://www.sla.org/membership/irc/copyright.html>.

Appendix G

Table of Cases

Kenneth D. Crews is a professor in the Indiana University School of Law-Indianapolis, with a joint appointment in the IU School of Library and Information Science. He is also director of IU's Copyright Management Center and serves as Associate Dean of the Faculties at Indiana University-Purdue University Indianapolis. Crews studied history at Northwestern University and received his law degree from Washington University in St. Louis. He practiced law in Los Angeles and earned a master's degree and Ph.D. in library and information science at the University of California, Los Angeles. His research centers on copyright and intellectual property issues of importance to educators and librarians.